HOW TO CRUSH IT IN BUSINESS WITHOUT CRUSHING YOUR SPIRIT

How Entrepreneurs Can Overcome Depression & Find Success

ELLEN VIOLETTE

INTERVIEWS WITH 17 INSPIRING ENTREPRENEURS

With the exception of brief quotations in review—with proper accreditation—no part of this ebook may be used, reproduced, or transmitted in any manner whatsoever without written permission from the author

Limits of Liability/Disclaimer of warranty:

The authors and publishers of this eBook and the accompanying materials have used their best efforts in preparing this book. The authors and publishers make no representation or warranties with respect to the accuracy, applicability, fitness, or completeness of the contents of this book. They disclaim any warranties (expressed or implied), merchantability, or fitness for any particular purpose.

Compiled by Ellen Violette

Published by Create a Splash
©Copyright 2017

All Rights Reserved
ellen@booksbusinessabundance.com
www.booksbusinessabundance.com

The authors and publishers shall in no event be held liable for any loss or other damages, including, but not limited to, special, incidental, consequential, or other damages.

As always, the advice of a competent legal, tax, accounting, or other professional should be sought. This book contains material protected under International and Federal Copyright Laws and Treaties. Any unauthorized reprint or use of this material is prohibited.

This book is for educational purposes only.

ISBN: 978-1707265-65-7

Cover Design: Nathanial Dasco
Inside Design: Carolyn Sheltraw
Edited by: Ellen Violette, Lizabeth Hall, & Jillian Wheeler

This book is dedicated to all the entrepreneurs out there who are working hard, trying to make a difference, taking risks and wondering if it's all worth it.

SPECIAL BONUS OFFER

You will receive completely FREE, two special reports to help you navigate through depression when you need it!

Click Here to Access Your two FREE reports
(If you have trouble with the link, you may access it directly at: www.overcomingdepressionforentrepreneurs.com/bonus-reports

1. *50 Reasons You Might Be Depressed in Your Business, Some Will Even Make You Laugh,* Special Report
   By Ellen Violette
2. *3 Universal Laws to Help You Deal with Depression* Special Report
   By Jillian Coleman Wheeler

Do the ups and downs of being an entrepreneur get you down at times?

Do you feel like you're alone and nobody understands what you're going through?

"50 Reasons Your Might Be Depressed in Your Business, Some Will Even Make You Laugh", identifies 50 reasons you might be depressed in a tongue and cheek sort of way to let you know we understand and there is a way to laugh at it!

"3 Universal Laws to Help You Deal with Depression" explains the three laws that are always in play and how you can use them to help you deal with depression when it arises.

Click Here to Access Your two FREE reports
(If you have trouble with the link, you may access it directly at: www.overcomingdepressionforentrepreneurs.com/bonus-reports

To join our Facebook Group: Overcoming Depression for Entrepreneurs for sharing, inspiration, support, and more, go to: http://www.Facebook.com/groups/overcomingdepressionforentrepreneurs

TABLE OF CONTENTS

Introduction 1

1. The Curse of Being Creative – Ellen Violette 7

2. How Can I Help Others When I Can't Do It Myself? – Benita Tyler 17

3. I Got the Music in Me – Julia Neiman 25

4. One Door Closed, Another One Opened – Gary Loper 33

5. I Just Have To Learn One More Thing… – Mary DeYon 43

6. Here Comes the Sun – Wayne Buckhanan 51

7. Money In, Money Out – Gerri Milligan 69

8. If You Do This It Will Happen…NOT –
   Kim Thornton 79

9. Rethinking My Life – Jillian Coleman Wheeler. 89

10. Alcohol, Depression & Faith – Willie Crawford 101

11. What's Wrong With Me? – Betsy M. Hall. 109

12. Success is a Team Sport – Rick Cooper. 115

13. Back to the Workforce, Really? – Brooklyn Reyes. . . . 125

14. What The Mind Can Believe, The Mind Can
    Achieve – Christen Violette 133

15. The Truth Shall Set Your Free – Mary Latela 141

16. Talking to an Angel – Joy Pedersen. 149

17. Businesses Come, Businesses Go –Rufina James. 157

Bonus Gifts from the Experts 167

Connect with the Experts 169

Resources. 179

Acknowledgements 181

About Ellen Violette. 183

INTRODUCTION

When I started my business online in 2004, everything fell into place pretty easily. I created a workbook, which is now called *The eBook-Writing Fast-Action Workbook*, which led to a two-part workshop on writing eBooks, which led to my very first *3 Days to eBook Cash Workshop* (one of my signature programs), and then my first marketing program, *eBook Profit Secrets*. I made $13,000 on that first marketing workshop and $47,000 that first year; I made a 6-figure income in 2 ½ years. We were living in Redondo Beach, California, in a two-story loft overlooking the ocean and driving a Silver C240 Mercedes with black interior that was absolutely gorgeous. Life was good!

And, we were on track to make $250,000 the next year. Then, the recession hit and the bottom fell out. I lost half of my business and had to sell almost all of the jewelry I had inherited from my mom (which was a lot!) plus, my 2 ½ carat platinum wedding ring. It was scary, and we didn't know if the business would survive.

I had gone from doing events that made me $16,000-$20,000 a pop, to losing money. And whereas prospects had been lining up to work with me, now it was hard work to get them in the door. The truth was that I had gotten online during the gilded age of the Internet where it was easy and you didn't have to be very good at it. Now, one had to understand the fundamentals of marketing and work at it.

So, I kept studying and trying different strategies and failing. Spending more money, buying more programs, and struggling. I still made money, but it wasn't easy and it wasn't fun any more. It wasn't just money that was eluding me, it was worse. It was happiness. I had become disillusioned and wasn't sure what I wanted. I started to question myself. Did I really want to build my business back the way it had been before? Or, did I want something else? And if so, what? And, how was I going to get it? My life became a roller-coaster ride of trying new things, deciding I didn't like them, quitting, and then trying something else. It was depressing and exhausting.

And to make matters worse, everyone on Facebook seemed to be doing so well. I found myself comparing myself to them and that just made it worse. Plus, my "friends" were getting tired of listening to me! I didn't mean to be negative, but I tend to over analyze things, and I was trying to figure it out by talking about it. Soon, my "friends" stopped coming around.

But, slowly the truth started seeping out. I'd hear whispering about other coaches and thought leaders who weren't happy either, complaining behind closed doors and crying themselves to sleep. And while I didn't wish them any ill will, I was relieved to find out that I was not the only one who was having a hard time.

Finally, I sat down and made a list of what I was passionate about, what skills I had, and what made me truly happy and realized that while I had set out with the right vision years earlier, somewhere along the line, I veered off the path and started listening to what other people were doing and the "best ways" to make money and I lost my way.

I'd also spent a lot of time helping other people build their dream lives while forgetting to plan and execute mine. So, I changed course and started doing more of what I wanted to do.

And one of the projects on my to-do list was a collaboration book. But, I didn't want to do just any collaboration book. It had to be something that I truly believed in and was different than all the other ones out there. I did not want to create another Chicken-Soup-for-the-Soul knock off.

So, I waited and waited until one day, I saw an article on Facebook about depression and entrepreneurs. It said that while 7% of the population was depressed in the United States, 49% of the entrepreneurs in this study were depressed. And according to Dr. Michael A. Freeman, a professor at the University of California, San Francisco 1 in 3 entrepreneurs suffers from depression.

And depression is a major cause of suicide. In fact, there is a long list of promising and well-known entrepreneurs who have committed suicide including 26-year-old Aaron Schwartz, a partner at Reddit, who hung himself in 2013, and 47-year-old Jody Sherman, founder of Ecomom, and the list goes on.

While this list of "successful" entrepreneurs who have killed themselves was shocking, it was not surprising to me given my own journey of entrepreneurship and bouts of depression along the way.

And that is what inspired me to create this book. I wanted to bring it out in the open, remove the guilt and shame that entrepreneurs feel for being depressed and feeling like they are alone and that nobody cares. I care and I want to support and help as many entrepreneurs as I can with this book.

As my #1 bestseller client and co-contributor to this book, Gerri Chambers, points out in her story, depression is not something that happens once in the life of most entrepreneurs, it is a fact of the entrepreneurial life that each one of us has to learn to handle over and over again in our quest to live the life of our dreams.

That is why I have dedicated this book to all the entrepreneurs out there who are willing to persist, overcome, and thrive in spite of all the trials and tribulations of entrepreneurship.

Hopefully this book will inspire you and guide you through your journey to the life you want and deserve.

THE CURSE OF BEING CREATIVE
BY ELLEN VIOLETTE

MY STORY

I have always been a creative person. I started keeping journals and writing poetry in junior high school. I took dance classes from the age of 5 until I graduated from high school. And while I tried to fit in by going to college and graduate school (in architecture), there came a point where I couldn't do it anymore. I was suffering from panic attacks and anxiety. I finally quit graduate school at the end of my second year, against the wishes of my family and boyfriend, got into therapy, and became a songwriter after my therapist suggested that my poems sounded like songs and maybe I should pursue it.

I was in the music business for 20 years and I loved every minute of it. My husband and I built a world-class studio in the house I grew up in, but when my parents both passed away within 11 months of each other, we had to sell the house. So, I lost the only way I had to make a living.

And to make matters worse, the house was earthquake damaged in the Northridge earthquake, so we had to fix it before we could sell it at a profit. So, my husband and I fixed the house and made quite a bit of money on it. It was at a time when the real-estate market was just starting to take off. We lived in Los Angeles at the time. But, we wanted a change of scenery once my parents were gone, so we moved down to San Diego. It was perfect timing. The real-estate market was just starting to move here, so we started buying, fixing and selling condos and houses.

We made almost a million dollars in a very short amount of time, but then the market got too hot, and there was nothing to buy that we could make money on. So, we went back to Los Angeles and that's when I got on the Internet and started networking locally. Since writing had always been one of my best skills, I started offering my copywriting services online.

But, I quickly realized that it wasn't something I wanted to do long term because each project took a lot of hours and too many of my clients didn't understand that what mattered was not if they liked it as much as whether it converted or not. Plus, I'd always wanted to write books.

So, I got on the Internet and started researching book writing. I found a New York Times Bestselling Author who critiqued my work, told me he thought it was good enough to make a living writing, and I should start sending my writing out on spec.

That was the last thing I wanted to do after being in the music business for 20 years prior to our real-estate years. In the music business, I got paid 10 cents a record while the artist and the publishers got rich, and I had absolutely no control over getting my songs cut. I didn't want to do that again. So, I started looking around online and found ebooks. And I'll never forget how excited I was! I ran out of my office shouting at my husband, that I had found eBooks and I was going to start writing them!

My first book was called *The Moving Cure, How to Organize Your Move to Save Time, Money & Your Sanity* and I was having difficulty learning how to write, publish, and market from a book. So, I went looking for an ebook coach and there weren't any. I hired a regular coach instead. It was expensive and inefficient. I would write, make mistakes, and then my coach would read it and tell me what I did wrong. I remember thinking that I could teach it better.

So, I did the research and put together my first program, *3 Days to eBook Cash*. It had a lot of good information in it, but it wasn't great. I kept working on it and improving it, until it was everything it should be. It is one of my signature programs; I have taught it to people all over the world, and it has changed lives.

And, I have gone on to create several other programs.

But, what I found was that I was always happier when I was creating something because it was new and different, and I could go at my own pace. But the marketing was always on a deadline, and it would stress me out.

So, I felt like I was on this merry-go-round of creating and enjoying it then rushing around feeling stressed out and exhausted, and then having to teach it. Then, the cycle would start all over again. Plus with each cycle, I would take on another new project to keep me interested. It was too much!

> **❝** I had to accept that as a creative I always want to be doing something creative, and I had to make room for that in any marketing plan and in my life without feeling guilty about it. **❞**

FINDING MY WAY OUT

I had to take a step back and look at what I really wanted and that was not easy. I would compare myself to other "successful" experts and feel like I SHOULD aspire to the same things they were doing, but it wasn't making me happy. So, I made a list of my skills AND what I enjoyed doing and decided to change my business model.

I also had to stop looking at all the shiny objects out there and spending so much time learning new things instead of focusing on the goals I wanted to accomplish myself. I had to put blinders on.

It definitely got easier once I got very clear on exactly what my goals were.

Then, I had to figure out how I was going to start doing more of what I wanted to do and less of what I didn't want to do.

Again, it wasn't easy. The key is outsourcing and automation, but you still have to stop what you're doing, find the right people, and teach them how to do the jobs you want done. You also have to set up automation, and then you have to test it and make sure it works; it's a process. And it's always easier to keep doing what you've been doing in the short run even though it's hurting you in the long run.

I also had to accept that as a creative I always want to be doing something creative, and I had to make room for that in any marketing plan, otherwise I would start to sink into a black hole.

And I had to accept that I am better at starting projects than finishing them for two reasons. First, I have a new idea about every five minutes and as a coach, I know that the latest idea is always the most exciting one and the one you want to work on, until the next one pops into your head and feels even better! And second, if you don't focus, you will start too many projects, and then get stressed out because they aren't finished on time.

And then, I had to start working on not being so hard on myself and this one has not been easy for me. Surrounding myself with loving support-people, who are there for me even when I can't quite get it together myself, has been really important for me and hanging out with successful people.

Then, I have my daily routine. I do affirmations and meditate every morning. And if I'm feeling really down, I whip out testimonials and notes that people have written me telling me how much I've helped them.

But, I also realized that I had certain patterns of thought and if I didn't break them, I was going to continue to make the same kinds of mistakes over and over, so I hired a coach to help me create new ways of thinking about my work and started doing EFT to break up old mental patterns.

I think you have to work on the business and on yourself if you want to get better so that is what I've done.

TIPS FOR OTHER ENTREPRENEURS

Getting clear about what you really want is key. Be totally honest with yourself or it won't work, and you won't be successful.

You may be doing what you think you should want to do or what others want you to do, so it can take some digging.

Then, find a business model that will get you the results that you have decided you want. One of the issues I had was that the business model I was following was never going to get me the results I wanted. It was a big shock when I realized that.

Also, the things I had done that worked really well became boring and repetitive. Those needed to be automated. I was making way too much work for myself for way too long; it was burning me out.

Get into a mastermind and, if you can afford it, get a coach. Many coaches are not as expensive as you think and are more accessible than you think. If you can't afford individual coaching find out how you can work with them another way until you turn the corner.

Also, realize that just because someone makes millions with a particular strategy doesn't mean you will be able to. You have to have a similar skill set and the right temperament to duplicate their results. So, make sure you have the right combination for the path that you choose. Plus, it is usually a lot more work than they say it is. So, be prepared to roll up your sleeves and do the work. And, never give up.

And then be sure to not only work on your business, but on yourself too. You have to grow to grow your business.

Ellen Violette helps Founders & CEO's, increase their influence in their respective industries through the process of creating a book, launching it #1 bestseller and using it to make an even bigger impact in the world.

She's an award-winning book and business coach, creator of several ground-breaking programs and courses, a 3-time eLit Award winner, former regular contributor to Published! Magazine, host of the Books Business Abundance Podcast, and a Grammy-nominated songwriter.

HOW CAN I HELP OTHERS WHEN I CAN'T DO IT MYSELF?
BY BENITA TYLER

MY STORY

I experienced depression back in 2008 during the economic downturn here in the United States. Many in our country were dealing with major losses in some form or another, and it had a ripple effect that hit my business.

I lost well over 60% of my income, and I'm the type of person who feels secure when I'm able to sock away savings. Plus, having stellar credit is icing on the cake. When my income took a hit, it not only impacted me, but it changed life for my whole household. My husband and I were both self-employed, and our lifestyle was based on a two-income household. So, faced so quickly with the loss, I questioned myself. I felt insecure about my ability to turn things around and successfully manage my finances. I just kept seeing myself as a failure.

It was not a good time for us. As an advisor to entrepreneurs, I felt like I was not in integrity. I kept asking myself, "How can I advise someone when the same thing is happening to me?" My self-esteem went out the window. My faith went out the window. With each passing day, I doubted myself more.

In spite of my desire to throw in the towel and climb under a rock, entrepreneurs were still reaching out to me; new prospects were still calling in. And, I still had my passion. But, during that time, it was only a little glimmer of light instead of this big one that shines through when I'm confident. I was turning away calls. I was turning away speaking engagements. I was turning away all types of opportunities and leaving money on the table because I just didn't have that confidence.

My message is about prospering in business, but I wasn't prospering in business. Because of that, it felt like "Who am I to go out and share this particular message with the world when I'm not even manifesting it in my own life?"

I had these big dreams to take my company global, but I couldn't think globally at the time. I couldn't even think past my living room!

The things that you think about actually manifest. All of those plans that I had for the live events and for writing… I couldn't wrap my mind around them because I couldn't focus and definitely couldn't go forth with any type of big plan.

❝ Any time I find myself in a stuck place, I reflect on that experience and ask myself, 'Where is the circle of people that stretches me or that holds me accountable?' ❞

FINDING MY WAY OUT

It went on for about three years, but then I connected to a friend who I hadn't spoken with during that time. And, it was odd, because she called me up out of the blue; it was just a "how-you-doing" type of conversation. And now, every time I see her I give her the biggest hug because she was my saving grace. God had sent me an angel.

She invited me out to attend a mastermind, and I went. That was the fuel that lit the fire again because being in something like that, being around people who are like-minded, not depressed, and really moving forward, was contagious; it brought me back to life.

I needed an environment where I could not only give value so that I could begin to feel like I was valuable, but also to be able to exchange ideas. That was literally what pulled me out.

Every time I look back on it, even when I get stuck today, I don't fall back into that type, or degree, of depression. Today, any time I find myself in a stuck place, I reflect on that experience and ask myself, "Where is the circle of people that stretches me or that holds me accountable?" Those types of things really, really matter.

Another thing was journaling. I was doing it before I became part of the mastermind group, but I wasn't journaling in a methodical way. It was more like a, "This-is-what's-happened-today" kind of thing. These days, I take a different approach. Instead of being completely free form, I have key points that I make sure to touch upon each time I sit down to write. I save the end of each session to capture anything else that's on my mind. I always make sure to include thoughts that make my life full.

TIPS FOR OTHER ENTREPRENEURS

My biggest tip, again, is connection. I always tell people, "You're not a one-woman or one-man island." We are created to connect with one another. It's the reason why having a mastermind, networking groups, or an inner circle, is so important. They exist for a reason, and they are one of the keys to living a full life. If you should ever get into a dark place, become stuck or confused, that's when inner circles will be very helpful to you.

And journaling, which is simply getting your thoughts out on paper, helps, too. I tried the computer, but it's just not the same. I needed to have the journal on my lap, a soft light, and a candle; it's the whole atmosphere that makes the difference.

So, even if you don't have anyone to talk to, the journaling process helps you to clear your mind, it starts the process of becoming aware of how you're truly feeling. For me, it was naturally therapeutic.

Several years ago, I learned from a life coach to fill my life with creativity. So, I find something each day that will help me to be creative. When I'm journaling, I'll write about my experiences... whether it's cooking a new dish, going to the local craft store, or seeing and writing about what I love about an art piece. Maybe it was a new color, or maybe it was the way the artist drew their experience, or how I interpreted it. Having those types of things is something that calms me and brings me to a place of peace.

That's probably one of my favorite parts of journaling. Also, because I start my day in prayer and meditation, I may write about a particular verse that stood out on the page and what it meant to me. Those are just some of the types of things that I do to keep my head on straight that may work for others.

Benita Tyler is officially known as "The Financial Messenger." Benita makes it her business to mind the business of others… literally. She was named as one of the top five people to watch by the Detroit Entrepreneur Institute, she coaches entrepreneurs worldwide in maintaining healthy cash flow and tax savings. It's her mission to help those whom she serves to build a legacy of wealth.

I GOT THE MUSIC IN ME
BY JULIA NEIMAN

MY STORY

I'm normally a really happy, easy-going person, but several years ago, I still had my job as a social worker, and I was creating a huge side project that didn't work out. I spent four years building it and bringing people together. The day we found somebody to fund us for $14 million—that's how big this project was—we were ecstatic!

But, this was back in 2008, when the economy plummeted, and the day they were supposed to deliver the check, they came to us and said, "We have bad news. We just lost a ton of money, and we're no longer able to fund this project."

I was in shock, and from that shock, I went into a huge depression. I had never experienced depression in my life before, ever-nothing like that. I was devastated, and it kept me down for a really, really long time.

To make matters worse, people who I thought would be supportive of me, who were not even connected to the project, but people in my life, tried to point out why it was my fault.

I called in sick to work for a whole week, and then I had to drag myself back to work. After a while, I thought, "You know what? I just can't live like this anymore, and I need help."

> Music really saved my life.

FINDING MY WAY OUT

I had had a long career as a clinical social worker, helping kids cope with depression, but none of those things were working for me in this situation, so I called an ethnomusicologist whom I knew; she does treatment with music. I said to her, "Elizabeth, I really need help, because I'm feeling depressed, and I need to do something." I thought, "I'm going to give music therapy a try."

She helped me create a therapeutic play list from the music I like, to help me modulate my moods. At her suggestion, I went out and bought a "Best of Bach", and played Bach concertos really low, like ambient background music that you're barely aware of-a whole CD of it-in a loop, 24 hours a day. These concertos create a certain energy frequency and cause the frequency around you to vibrate at a different level that lifts you out of depression. It makes you feel really good, even if you're not aware that it's in the background.

I noticed after 48 hours, I started to feel better. I attributed it to the music. Then, she sat with me, and we picked out some personal choices of music that I liked the best and played them. She said, "When you're feeling angry over this, get some music that expresses that anger, and let the music express that for you, so that you don't have to hold it inside."

Most people can't help but sing along to music, or bounce around in your chair, or whatever it is you do when music is playing. Music, because of the vibration of the sound waves, has an effect on you, both on your emotional body and your physical body.

I say music really saved my life, because if I had stayed in this depression … I'm a Pisces, and when we have our lows, we have really low lows, I may never have gotten out of it. It really did bring me back into the world of the living, because I just wanted to go to bed and never get up again. I can't recommend it highly enough.

Then when I started to feel better, what I did was something that I always recommended to my own clients. I kept a "thought diary". I kept track of my thoughts, especially the negative ones. I would always look at those, and then try to find out what triggered them, because for weeks, it was like I was in the grieving process, grieving the loss of that project, along with being devastated and feeling depressed over it.

This was going to support foster-care kids transitioning out of foster care, and transform a lot of lives. It wasn't just a loss to me personally, but it was the loss of a dream for all of these kids, and the things that I wanted to help them with; I wanted to transform transitional living projects in the foster-care system, and really give these kids hope for the future. I saw all that flush down the drain with the rest of the economy.

So between the music, and keeping track of my thoughts, because I firmly believe that we create our reality with our thoughts, I got better.

I had been so depressed, and unaware. I really needed to raise my level of awareness of what I was doing to myself, because there comes a point in time where you have to take responsibility for what you're feeling. What we feel from one minute to the next is a choice, and I just made the decision that I was going to feel better, and I wasn't going to let that keep me down.

From that minute on, I started to become more aware of what I was thinking, and I transformed that into more positive thoughts every time I would catch it. I found that it opened a whole new level of awareness for me, and I never went backwards from that point on. It turned everything around.

TIPS FOR FIGHTING DEPRESSION

I think that it's a really good thing to reach out to people to help you. When you're depressed, don't try to hide it. A lot of people try hiding it by putting on a cheery facade.

People know something is wrong, but they don't really want to ask you what's going on. If you just tell somebody, "I'm feeling really depressed, and I could use support from you. It's nothing special, but if you hear me being negative, or you see my energy level bottoming out, would you just point it out to me, so that I could focus my awareness on what's going on?" I think with that kind of support it makes a huge difference.

But, you have to reach out to people that you really trust. They don't have to have anything to do with your business, and they probably shouldn't.

That was a rude awakening in my life, too—looking at the people who tried to bring me down more by telling me all the things that I did wrong that made this happen when it wasn't anything I did. Needless to say, these people were not in my life after that. Even the money guy kept saying to me, "This isn't anything you did. We love this project, and we feel terrible about this."

I was never clinically depressed. It was purely emotional. It wasn't the kind of thing that any kind of medication would've helped. I was just going through the grieving process, and in that process, the depression became really overwhelming until, as I said, I started using the music to change.

Keep in mind, it really is about a choice. If you choose to be happy, then you will take action to be happy, and that makes all the difference.

Julia Neiman, MSW, is an international bestselling author, youth entrepreneurship coach, and creator of Monetize Your Passion Academy *with more than 20 years working with disenfranchised teens,*

Julia experienced first hand the life-altering turnarounds achieved when teens are supported in monetizing their passions. Today, she is passionate about sharing these steps to entrepreneurial success with all persons. Julia has been heard on radio interviews both nationally and internationally as well as in print.

She is an ambassador for and currently serves on the Board of Directors of Parenting 2.0's educational nonprofit, The Global Presence and as Vice President and Secretary of Mountain Radio, Inc. She is the host of the new Monetize Your Passion Radio Show *(soon to be podcast). Julia lives in Agua Dulce, California, the foothills to the high desert in Los Angeles County.*

ONE DOOR CLOSED; ANOTHER ONE OPENED
BY GARY LOPER

MY STORY

I grew up in a household where my mom struggled with depression, but at the time, I didn't realize that she was depressed. She was either in bed all the time or in a housecoat, and did *not* function well. As a rule, she didn't go with us to family events. So, that type of DNA-seed planting was already present. Over time, I recognized that when I had major events going on in my life, like after my divorce, a long-term breakup, or a job loss, I would get locked down. I began to recognize my reaction and actions in hindsight rather than at the time of the actual occurrence.

The last time it happened was in November 2008. My awareness strengthened, and things began to unfold.

About three years earlier, I did massage for special-needs clients, working with people with cerebral palsy, schizophrenia, Tourette's, and a lot of other diseases. I went into their homes a couple of times a week; I made an incredible impact in their health.

One client was able to get off of his meds because of the massage work I did with him. And, it also filled me up emotionally. Since I was emotionally driven, the money wasn't a huge motivating factor. Working with special-needs clients was my enthusiasm. Subsequently, because I was in their homes several times a week, I connected emotionally with my clients and their families.

At one point, there were rumors going around that the funding for this program was going to be eliminated. Nonetheless, we didn't believe it was going to happen, because the program was so effective; our work was making a difference.

But then, in November of 2008, the entire program was eliminated, so all that income was gone as well as all that emotional support. It was devastating. I fell onto the couch for a long period of time and couldn't do anything.

> **❝ Starting to be of service to other people changed everything. ❞**

FINDING MY WAY OUT

One way I shifted my energy was through Twitter. Initially, I started using Twitter simply to explore the possibilities. My motivating factor was to get myself up off of the couch. I remembered that I had studied personal development in 1989, and I had collected a lot of motivational quotes. I started reading the collection of quotes to lift my depression. Then, I began to share those messages. And in sharing those messages, people began to respond. They were asking questions. They were thanking me. They were retweeting me.

That was the beginning of my shift. And, that's when I first tapped into: *"Gary, you've been a coach since 1999. Now, you're going to start coaching. This will be your next chapter, and you're going to use Twitter as a vehicle to be able to achieve that."* That was really the beginning of the solution phase.

I wanted to make a positive impact in the world. Shifting the focus off of me, getting into my stories, putting the focus out there, and starting to be of service to other people changed everything.

At that point, I started to create a series of *#JustForToday* affirmations, simple messages to help shift your thoughts in a positive direction. In my effort to help the Twitterverse, I began to write hundreds of affirming thoughts and share them using the hash tag *#JustForToday*. They are little daily reminders of what we need when we're down or depressed. We can't go out there, flip a switch, and go from depression to joy. The more positive messages you fill your head and heart with, the easier it is to make that shift.

An example of a *#JustForToday* affirmation would be: *Just for today I'm going to turn the TV off.* Remember they are simple, little reminders that can be built up over time. Within 60 to 90 days, you create a new habit.

The *#JustForToday* affirmations made a massive impact on me, which in turn inspired me to put out daily motivational messages on every stream. Affirmations are great!

To add to that, a powerful and heartfelt event occurred on Twitter one day. A few years ago, a young lady wrote to me on Twitter. She said, "I could never thank you enough for what your tweets have done for me." So I asked her to email me, to tell me more about it. She told me that she was dealing with a debilitating disease, and because of the pain and everything else she was going through, she was contemplating suicide, until one of those *#JustForToday* affirmations showed up in her Tweet stream. She changed her mind and decided to stay. She made a decision to work with her disease, and to help other people with the same condition.

Those daily recognitions and that story, knowing that I can make a difference and make an impact, gave me the validation that I needed. And, I know that putting those messages out there is a butterfly effect. They're going to reach the people who need it, when they need it, and it's going to make a difference in their world in one way or another. I am just blessed to know that impact happened.

That's been a shift where I can stay on top of those depressed feelings.

TIPS FOR OTHER ENTREPRENEURS

A lot of times, you have to change the story that you're telling yourself and change the questions that you ask. I learned that if you ask the universe, "Well, why is this happening to me? Woe is me," then your subconscious mind and the universe will play all the reasons why it's happening to you. Instead ask, "How do I get stronger? How can I be better, so I don't react this way?"

Here is a vital tip: Remove all the negative people, and the negative news from your life. If you're feeling sad, you don't need to hear negative or sad stories. Turn off the news for 60 days. If there is something you need to know, someone will come and tell you.

But, it's more important to turn off the negative people in your life. And, there are ways that you can do it.

1. Put **DNA** (do not answer) into your phone. Let's say Debbie is calling you, and you know that Debbie is an energy vampire, she'll take you off track and bring you down into a ditch. Put **DNA** in front of her name to remind you **do not answer**. This way you can control whether or *not* you're going to call her back, or choose *not* to call her back at all. If you don't call her

back, she'll go find somebody else to go vent to. That's what vampires do.

2. When you go to family gatherings, your family loves you, but probably *not* in a way that you always want. So, if you tell them about your dreams, especially as entrepreneurs, they may discourage you.

It's your responsibility to protect your dream, because they're probably going to, in their way of loving, say, "Well, we knew somebody who did that, and it didn't work for them." It can be really deflating.

So, here's how I deal with this when I am asked, "How's your business?" My response is, "Unbelievable." Because if it sucks, it's unbelievable. If it's great, it's unbelievable. Then, shift the conversation off to somebody else. Don't let them in if you know that they're going to burst your bubble. They're *not* going to validate you.

3. Upgrade your associations. Look for people who've already traversed that depression angle. Look to Ellen and me, and other people who are telling their stories in this book. Talk to people who are getting out of it and know how to get out of it.

Otherwise, it's like a crab trap. Those other people are going to pull you back into the trap and *not* let you out.

4. Follow me on Twitter. Get a dose of positive information whenever you can. If you look at collecting a bunch of positive people around you, it's bound to rub off. Their belief in you will establish your belief in yourself. I think that's why we get depressed. We don't believe in ourselves enough, and we don't have confidence. We need support, and we need other people who understand what we're feeling or what we're going through.

Those are the huge ones. But again, probably the biggest thing is having faith about that seed of good in every situation. A metaphor that I use all the time is: There's a pony in the poop. What do the farmers do all the time with all the poop and the manure? They use fertilizer. They plant the seed. They turn the soil over, and they spread that poop over the fertilizer, so it nurtures the new seed.

So, make a vow to yourself that you're going to plant that new seed, and you're going to use those past experiences for fertilizer to make your new dream, your new path, flourish.

Gary Loper has dedicated every day of the past 25 years to personal development. His lifelong enthusiasm and passion is to assist individuals in becoming their best.

Gary is a social media expert specializing in Twitter training. Times have changed; no longer are customers wooed by commercials and pitches; they are looking for relationships they can feel good about. Gary can help you navigate this new marketing world to grow your business and live your dream.

Gary has a strong background in marketing and sales with 30+ years of customer service and 15 years of direct sales and social media.

I JUST HAVE TO LEARN ONE MORE THING...
BY MARY DEYON

MY STORY

When I worked in sales, I always made a lot of money and even received many awards for being the best salesperson. But what depressed me when I began my business was all the money was going out and none was coming back in. When I realized this, I really hit bottom.

I began my new Internet business while I was still working in sales, because my job was being phased out, so I needed a new career. I was trying to learn online marketing and all the other things that I needed to know to have a successful online business, but I got too far away from what I instinctively knew inside myself.

I kept thinking, "The next guru will know what I need," so I was attending a lot of seminars, and I was driving myself crazy. They said I needed to write this and do that program. I was running myself ragged going in too many directions. I got into a deeper depression.

I was spending so much money trying to launch this new business, and I wasn't making any money, so my confidence and self-worth went down the tubes. I felt really inadequate.

> I finally listened to my inner guidance and got back into what I originally wanted to do.

FINDING MY WAY OUT

I finally listened to my inner guidance and got back into what I originally wanted to do. Before, I was listening to everybody else. I even had a business coach and she had great ideas—but it wasn't what I originally planned to do. Once I tuned in, the ideas started coming.

When I wasn't making money I would start my day with a cup of coffee, head to the computer, and I'd be stuck there all day working, and working, and working.

When I finally went back to honoring myself and getting up in the morning, spending some quiet time of reading and meditating, and getting in that centered place, the good ideas came to me.

Before, I was doing too much outward stuff and stuck at my computer, I wasn't even exercising. But when I got back into doing some yoga, dancing, or taking a walk, everything improved. I remembered energy techniques I had used for 40 years and began taking care of me, instead of always trying to do what everybody said I was supposed to do.

TIPS FOR OTHER ENTREPRENEURS

Take care of yourself. Find the right food that works for you and gives you energy all day long. There are so many diet gurus out there who say, "Do this, do that." Find out what works for YOU!

I think exercise is huge in fighting depression. If I don't do some kind of movement every day, I could go back in the dumpers really easily. Do what you like. I'm not a gym person, but if that's you, great. I've fallen off treadmills and popped out ribs lifting too much. So, it's not for me. Once you find out what works for you, stick to it.

When you're depressed, it's hard to get to the point to actually take action, but once you take that action, it works to move you forward!

Just remember, whenever you start something new the resistance shows up. Expect it. Think about this: you start going to the gym and you have another obligation that you need to attend to, and it interrupts your schedule. It becomes really easy to miss the next trip to the gym, and then the next. Then, you beat yourself up and never go back. Remember this is normal. Don't let this stop you from taking care of yourself.

Another thing that really helped me tons was getting rid of clutter all over my house, not just my office. Face the pile of unopened bills, the pile of papers that need something done with them that pile of dry cleaning that needs to go to the cleaners. Clean out your purse and your car. Do your dishes and the laundry, because every time you walk by them your energy drops.

One of the first steps in feng shui is to clear clutter because a cluttered space represents a cluttered mind and will cause depression. If you are constantly looking at all the things you have to do, it's exhausting. When money is not coming in, you freak out. But when you clear out all the clutter, your mind becomes free. Then, you are much more open to new ideas to make money.

And, get to your happy place every single morning as I mentioned earlier. It's the first rule of the law of attraction: like attracts like. I call it a "good hair day." You know, when your hair looks good, the world is sunny and bright because you're in that happy place. And, magically everything falls into place that day.

This morning attitude shift has helped many of my clients. I do think most salespeople wake up in the morning and the first thing they do is check their phone and email and that decides how their day will go. They are off and running. I say, "Okay, after you've done that and you've settled your mind, take the time to clear your mind. Read the Bible or meditate, listen to music—whatever it takes to get to your "happy place."

Next, make sure you're having fun. People don't want to do business with people who aren't fun.

Realize that every single time you start something new, resistance will show up. You start with this big resolve and you're in the fairytale castle, and you're surrounded by concrete. You are firm. This time you're going to do it, right? But what you don't realize is that right outside the castle are all the dragons on the other side of the moat. And they come in the form of procrastination, perfectionism, and self-sabotage. Realize that this will happen.

Instead of beating yourself up and letting it become a downward spiral, you say to yourself, "Okay, something got in the way today, but it's not going to stop me tomorrow." Get back on the horse. Don't let this derail you. When we break promises to ourselves, it's especially bad. So, make commitments to yourself and keep them.

We can do all these things, but many times people will still feel depressed. What they don't realize is that their subconscious mind in holding onto trapped emotions or limiting beliefs that are causing the depression. These emotions can even come in your DNA from your ancestors. I do energy healings that remove these blocks to people's success. So, if you aren't finding your way out of the depression on your own, you may want to explore other options.

Mary DeYon is an accomplished author, business coach and energy healer. She's a Certified Emotion Code Practitioner and certified Reiki Master. Mary has worked with energy for over four decades and focuses on removing the trapped emotions that block success in reaching your financial, relationship and health goals. Her clients have rapidly overcome depression and anxiety to achieve abundance and joy. Her unique approach is done with humor and compassion while being non-invasive, intuitive and empowering.

HERE COMES THE SUN
BY WAYNE BUCKHANAN

MY STORY

It took me years to figure out just how much the weather impacts my mood. This isn't the "I'm sad when it rains" sort of impact. This is breakdowns and depression after months of dreary winter weather. I've never actually been diagnosed with seasonal affective disorder (SAD), but my experiences sure fit with what I've read about SAD.

What this means is that if I'm not careful, I'll end up wrestling with the depression that is hiding in the shadows. It is easier to fall into a funk due to months of overcast skies here in the Midwest, but it has snuck up on me at other times and places, as well.

I first noticed the pattern in my life decades ago. Through my college years, I had a rhythm of going somewhere sunny and being physically active about every other year. There were trips to California to rollerblade in the San Francisco Bay Area and short-term mission trips to Honduras and Venezuela to do construction work. It wasn't until I went a couple years without one of these sorts of breaks that I realized how big of an impact they really made on my outlook.

Soon after I got married, I had quit an unsatisfying job and was enjoying some time away from a 40-hours-a-week desk job. The business I'd had as a side hustle had hit a lull, and business was slow. That's when I started feeling extra low. I look back and realize that I was in the prime of my life; I was married to this wonderful woman and rather than living up to my potential, I found myself lurking in the basement and distracting myself on the Internet—back before there was any YouTube or Facebook.

Somehow, I managed to get a new job, and we bought our first house while I was still in a funk. Oh, sure, things seemed to get better, and I guess they really were. Obviously, things weren't all peachy with the stresses of being newly married, dealing with a mortgage for the first time, and keeping my business moving forward while holding down a day job. But, this was about the time that I discovered NLP.

Neuro-Linguistic Programming (NLP) is one of those sprawling terms that gets attached to a lot of things and confused with a lot more. When I stumbled into the wrong part of the Internet one day, I found these people using language patterns (which I love) to coerce women at the clubs into bed (which was so far from my reality, I almost rejected NLP entirely). I backed out of that dark alley on the Internet and wondered how people could think that PUA (pick-up artists) and NLP stuff would make them happy.

Thankfully, the next time I ran into NLP, it was in a better context, and my love for playing with words hooked me. (I'm fairly sure that learning NLP saved my marriage. Between delving deeper and deeper into the cognitive psychology behind NLP and continuing to develop flexibility in my language and behaviors, we're now happily married for 17 years and counting.)

So, yeah, at the time, things were looking up a little, which is why it never really hit me that I was still fighting depression through it all. But another year just sitting behind a desk with no direct sunlight took its toll, and I had a breakdown.

My breakdown was one of those tears and snot episodes. I remember sitting on the edge of my bed just sobbing because I couldn't do it any more-sitting in the cubicle for my day job, chasing down uninterested prospects in my business, and doing things that I hated in both. So, I made the decision to quit my job. I just wanted to be happy and successful, but if that's what success looked like, I was not keen on that at all.

There I was, with no real plan and no idea where I was going with my life.

FINDING MY WAY OUT

After I had my breakdown and quit my job, one of my friends who taught sociology at the college level said, "Hey, do you want to come talk to my class?" I said, "Sure, what about?" He said, "We're talking about how people feel like a cog in the machine." I said, "Yes, I can definitely talk about that!"

I talked to his class; it was fun; we hung out. It was new, and I was out of the house in a new place. So, I asked if they needed anybody else to teach. Two months later, I was teaching at the college level. It turned out to be one of the best things I'd ever done. I spent four-and-a-half years teaching at that college before I went back for my PhD, so that I could keep teaching.

That breakdown and the shifts that followed changed my life.

It really made it clear to me that SAD is a real thing. Those years spent trapped in a cubicle were just the sort of environment the depression needed to rear its ugly head. I had stopped exercising, was barely getting any sunshine during the week, and then was hiding inside on the weekends, too.

Of course, humans can be stubborn beasts, and I had to go through the same patterns again in grad school to really learn the lesson. Eventually, I learned that I needed to be more conscious of the patterns and pay more attention to what's going on behind the scenes in my life.

My grad-school battle with depression got worse the farther along I got and the more intensely I focused on school to the exclusion of everything else. Since "everything else" included my business, I decided to take some time off from my studies and focus on getting my business growing again. Guess what? Depression said "Nope. No, you're not."

Through a random chain of events (that included finding out I have many ADD symptoms, but good coping mechanisms), I ended up seeing a counselor about the depression. That was enough of a nudge to get me headed in the right direction, and my NLP background took over.

I had to decide what I really wanted in life. Did I really want to finish the Ph.D and teach? Did I really want my business to take off? As it turned out, yes, I did. So, I started getting things done to move them forward.

Within a couple of months, I defended my Ph.D and had a teaching job waiting for me in California. I thought, "Geez, it only took me a decade to figure out how to manage my depression." And while my years in the "wilderness" of California weren't all sunshine and redwoods, I have gotten much better at catching myself early when I'm on the descent, so I can stay out of the dark depths.

One of the things that seemed to make a difference for me was getting a professional involved. The last time around, it was a simple coaching session where I was able to articulate one of my major blocks that was cycling with the depressive tendencies. I spotted it, said "Duh, there's a pattern." I broke out of it, and my business began to thrive again.

But sometimes, you really do need full-on counseling. I have friends who rely on their counseling and medications to regulate their moods. I'm glad I have managed without meds, since I know I am stubborn and am unlikely to actually take them based on my personality. I'm also glad my friends are in good spirits because of their meds. Whichever way you lean, counseling is something to consider even in the short term.

Since I have had struggles that seem to follow the seasons, I started paying more attention to how much sunshine I am getting—no matter what time of year it is. I found that in addition to getting outside, I needed to keep track of how much I was moving and exercising. I finally hired a personal trainer once a week and have developed a cadence of various workouts through the week that seem to be working for me.

As much as I need metaphorical "butt-in-seat" time for my writing, I paid for it physically and mentally. So, I got myself a standing desk that gives me more chances to move and sway throughout the day. I have a tall chair available, too, but find that I am much more likely to get stiff joints and sore muscles sitting than standing. Oh, and I found that once I got the ergonomics right and got my monitors up high enough, my neck and shoulders are able to release the tension that otherwise accumulates there when I'm stressed. There is something metaphorically satisfying about having to keep my chin (and outlook) up while working.

Another option is having multiple workspaces whether that is having some time in the home office versus at a cafe or library, or even just having multiple places I can work from within my office. Even moving a few feet away to another working surface is better than being fixed in one place for long hours.

I also have my favorite tools for exercise on hand in my workspaces for breaking up intense work sessions. In my case, that is a chunk of metal: kettle bells or club bells. They are small enough to tuck under a chair or in a corner to be available. And even 30 seconds of swings with a heavy bell is enough to raise my heart rate and break the monotony of desk time while also doing a little to fend off the depression.

And, yes, I get it. If you're feeling at all down or depressed, you probably don't want to exercise. You may not even want to eat well. That's why you make it as small a commitment as possible. Long before I heard of Tiny Habits®, I wrote a report on "MnM goals" -minimum, normal, maximum goals. (I'll include that in the bonus downloads that you get with this book.) The core idea is that while you may want to set these huge goals, you have to start where you are and set up the minimum action that will send you in the right direction. (You'll find it through the Bonus Gifts Section of this book.)

As entrepreneurs reading this book, we face the double whammy of working long hours along with a likely predisposition towards depression. You may find yourself working against the depression to get moving, even though you know that moving more will help alleviate the depression. That's where those minimum movements come into play.

While you may really want your norm to be 3-5 hours a week of intense exercise, anything is better than nothing! One push up. One squat at your standing desk. One flight of stairs before getting on the elevator. It all helps. And, it also makes it more likely you'll do a second push up, squat, or flight of stairs while you're there.

There are also the indirect methods. Want to increase your step count? Drink more water. (You'll need to visit the facilities that much more often!) You'll also fend off any dehydration that may be making things worse, both physically and mentally. These are all indirect benefits of a simple habit you can develop—one sip at a time.

Speaking of step counts… I picked up a simple Fitbit tracker. It gave me a good idea of just how low my baseline step count really was—a measly 2500 steps on an average day at my desk writing and in the classroom training. It also showed me what days I hit the recommended minimum of 10,000 steps in a day—and at first, it was only when I went shopping. Even without doing anything unusual in my life, all of a sudden I noticed how I could add a bit more movement just by volunteering to pick up the groceries more often.

Besides the physical aspects of sunshine, movement, and water intake, the thing I've done for myself that make the biggest difference day-to-day is noticing my self-talk. Bonus points when you change things up after you notice the self-talk, but first things first: pay attention to what you're telling yourself!

When things are at their worst, you don't see the light at the end of the tunnel. Or sometimes, you see the light and tell yourself it is an oncoming train. That mindset of "life is horrible" is part of what makes life horrible. There is that part of your brain that says something little and tells you, "See, it's exactly like I said it was" and all of a sudden you're self-reinforcing the cycle.

Don't stay there spinning downward for too long or eventually you start to believe it—even the part of you that knows it isn't true. That part can get drowned out and shut down because you had that negative record on repeat.

For example, I had a real-estate deal where I was getting strung along for years. We had a verbal agreement, and I could never get them to put it into writing. I was upset at the situation, obviously, but at some point I was able to step back and realize it was more than just righteous indignation. The sneaky depression DJ had snuck some tracks into the playlist that were making it worse.

My breakthrough on that situation came the day I realized I wasn't willing to take a particular action because it would make the other person look like they had done the "right thing" three years into the situation. I was able to notice that self-talk and realize that I could have anything I wanted if I would just let them "be right." I immediate caught myself saying I needed to write them a letter telling them I'm doing things *in spite* of their actions, not because of them. I laughed as soon as I realized even that was me having to "be right!"

These are the subtle sorts of self-talk that nudge us in the wrong direction. And by "wrong," I mean in unhelpful ways.

I'd much rather spend a few minutes setting up some more productive directions in my self-talk and building up a habitual internal dialogue that supports what I want to do rather than undermining it.

The crazy thing is that I've spent a dozen years studying and practicing these sorts of language patterns and working with belief structures and I still get derailed occasionally! We all get caught up in our own patterns and beliefs at times. Taking the time to notice them is the first step.

All the tools in the world don't help you when you get so caught up in life that you don't see what you're repeatedly doing or hear what you're consistently saying to yourself. But then, once you notice it, you can use all the tools you have to get you out of the mud as elegantly as possible.

TIPS FOR OTHER ENTREPRENEURS

I can't recommend highly enough working on your observational skills and developing a bit more flexibility in what we say to ourselves and others.

Now, am I suggesting that we get rid of every negative thought? No. For one, "getting rid of" is negatively phrased. But deeper still, we seem to be wired to pay attention to the negatives. If you look at it through the metaphor of evolution, you've got to pay attention to the things that can hurt you like saber-toothed tigers.

It turns out, you probably also want to avoid thinking about them surprising you all the time because our bodies are built to respond to those one-off surprises, but not a constant feeling of dread. Our modern stressors tend to be lingering thoughts that we play and replay. And dealing with depression seems to make it that much easier to get stuck in a debilitating loop or even drain the joy from enjoyable aspects of life.

So, just think happy unicorn-and-rainbow thoughts, right? Well, sort of. There is a big difference between not lingering on the "negative" and the sickly-sweet version of positive thinking that forbids acknowledging anything we don't like. The fact that we label something as negative already tells us it is likely to contain some useful information about the world as we see it.

Rather than an optimist/pessimist sort of world view, I find that focusing on developing an internal focus of control gives more benefits. This is about paying attention to the aspects of life that you can control and acknowledging those aspects you can't control. While optimists only seem to see the up-sides and pessimists only seem to see the down-sides, that sense of control allows you to see the world more clearly and do what you can to make it a better place—and acknowledging the saber-toothed tigers when they show up.

An optimist sees a pothole in the driveway and thinks "Spring is coming soon!" A pessimist sees the same pothole and grumbles about how much they hate winter and how bad their alignment will be from the hole. I see it and start problem solving to fill in the pothole, so it has the least amount of impact (no pun intended, for once). I'm using the information I have available—not fixated on the problem or ignoring it because it is "negative."

Plus, if all you ever do is run away from things that hurt you, your life has no direction. You need to tie in the "away from" that gets you moving with a "towards" that set a direction. In NLP circles, this is called a propulsion system. It is like a rocket to Mars. First, you have to get away from the Earth, and then you can focus on going toward Mars. But if all you can think is "not this" and "not that," you need to take a step back and figure out what you really do want.

Again, these are things that are difficult when in the throes of depression. This is why you want to dig your well before you're thirsty.

By the time you get into a situation and wish you had a better way to respond, it is generally too late to think about what other response you'd prefer. Unless you can guarantee you'll have the mental and/or physical space to step out of the situation, it is something you want to do ahead of time.

One of the skills you'll want to develop is setting up triggers before you'll need them. Everyday life seems to present us with lots and lots of triggers that fire off states that we could do without—road rage, apathy, and other states that can lead to depression or just make it worse. Instead, you'll want to use those same triggers to fire off resourceful states of mind.

One technique for doing this type of state control involves noticing the earliest hints that you're headed in a direction you don't like and changing directions while it is easier. One of the other pieces included in the bonuses section mentioned in the back of this book is a worksheet and an audio where I walk you through the process of intentionally setting up your triggers to take you where you'd prefer to go. The great part is that it is ridiculously simple little things that you probably already know how to do that you probably just haven't thought to apply in this particular way.

Another issue that comes up for entrepreneurs, and especially for the people working primarily online, is finding people to connect with in the real world. When you give up the 9-to-5-office job, you are also giving up the casual interactions around the water cooler and at lunch. I even know entrepreneurs with physical offices and employees who fall into the trap of being "the boss" and unintentionally shut themselves off from the human contact.

Especially when feeling depressed, it can be really hard to reach out. That's why it is a good idea to be building the network and nurturing those connections before you fall into the deep pit. Hopefully, if you've been down in the dumps, you've got a good enough network that someone will come and say, "Hey, are you okay down there?" At that point, you can use the nudge to start getting yourself out of the funk.

The thing to remember here is that as much as you don't want to interact with people, that's exactly what you need. Laughter is a great mood adjuster. Faith groups can provide spiritual support. Hanging out with people is important. I have a group that I regularly play geeky board games with, and if someone's been having a rough week, we are there to give them a boost.

Sitting in the corner while people are having fun around you is a reasonable start if that's all you can manage. Just being in that physical space can have a big impact—especially for those of us who sit behind a computer a lot. That face-to-face human contact is one of the best forms of support I've come across.

Second best is to make sure you're talking to your online friends. Get on Skype or Hangouts or Zoom with folks for casual conversations. Do whatever you need to do in order to interact more. Network with people who have the ability to make you laugh, to bring out your joy, and to help you see the ridiculousness of the things you're doing to yourself. When you take a break from beating up on yourself and are able to laugh at the same behaviors instead, that's powerful medicine.

And the same idea with movement: use any prompt you can to get moving. Set an alarm on your phone. Schedule breaks. Meet up with someone to walk at lunch. Do whatever you have to do in order to remind yourself to eat well, drink enough fluids, and make sure you're moving. It all makes a difference and supports us in getting out of the pit.

Dr. Wayne Buckhanan is a tech geek who loves people and teaching. He applies his PhD in electrical engineering while teaching engineering and computer science at the university level, leverages his two decades of business experience teaching innovation and entrepreneurship, and uses his studies of cognitive behavioral psychology and adult developmental models in the training and professional coaching disciplines. He's a licensed trainer of Applied Neuro Synergy, NLP, ChangeWorks ®, and instructional design.

MONEY IN, MONEY OUT
BY GERRI MILLIGAN

MY STORY

I was laid off from a job I had had for five years. I went right into another job that I knew didn't feel right. But, I worked there for nearly five months. Then, I got laid off. It was in oil and gas; it was a little iffy; it wasn't a good fit anyway, so it was the perfect time for me to say, "Okay. I'm not going to go back into the workforce."

I had 401K, I had some savings, and I thought I could slip into this Internet world and just kill it. That was the confidence level I had. I put up quite a bit of money on training, tools, and software, and I was heading to the point where I hadn't received any money back. You invest and invest.

When you have no money coming in and you're draining your savings, and you're watching that go, and you have four children to take care of, it's a little nerve-racking.

I'm a really optimistic person, so I had the mindset right, I had the optimism, and I had the go-getter attitude, the whole thing. It took a little while, about 2014 ... toward the end of 2014 when I really started to get scared that I was not going to make any money doing this. The 401K was gone, not to mention being taxed up the wazoo for that. Then, the savings was gone and I started dipping in to my son's college funds, but I was going to make this work because I am a winner.

I had decided to homeschool my children, so I had three boys at home, all pre-teenage and a newborn. There was an insurmountable amount of pressure on me to provide. I was stuck between providing the way I wanted to, which was to do my own thing, or going back out in the workforce, which would have really gone against what I wanted to do.

I came to a place where I hit rock bottom. I was really depressed. I did not fall into a decade of depression as some do. But it was a bout of depression that immobilized me, so I couldn't do anything. There was no productivity.

My children saw me kind of fold under. They didn't know what to do, which fed again into a depression that, "Great. Not only am I not producing, not only probably am I going to have to go back into the workforce, which is what I don't want to do. But now my children are seeing me crumble and not succeed." So, it was a culmination of things. It ultimately led to some immobility and basically just crawling up into a ball in the corner and just quitting.

You get back up again, well that's me. I just get back up again, whether it was connecting with someone who was very motivating, or someone who had made it or been there. You try to plug back in. I'm not going to completely give up on life; I knew that I had to keep going for my children.

I got back up and plugged back into some motivating people and people who had kind of been there, just started over again. I would go at it full force and fail again-what I saw as failure at the time. It just took me right back down. It felt like a faster cycle, so it was up for a minute, then back down another two days. Then, back up for a second, for a day, then back down for another couple of days. It came in shorter spurts. I remember calling people and crying, saying, "I'm going to just go ahead and quit now."

When people come to people desperate; you want people to help pick you up. That's what I got. People would say, "You've got what it takes. Keep going, just do it again. Do these three things.

So, I had those moments of getting back up again, but nothing was producing. So, I'd try again, and spend more money, and it was down again.

> ❝ it's a constant process of keeping yourself up because no one is going to hold your hand. No one is going to come pick you up and take you to work. ❞

FINDING YOUR WAY OUT

There were always actionable things that people told me to do.

One is just to focus on one thing that you can be successful at; it may be a very small thing. So, it may be just getting up in the morning. Honestly, if you are that down, getting up and brushing your teeth is a big deal.

Really, it was just going out and taking a walk. I mean people would literally tell me to get outside your house and go walk around the block. Go smell some fresh air and look at some flowers. I remember doing that a couple times. I knew my children were going to see me in a really bad position, so I just walked out of the house.

They also told me to complete one task for my business. Not to look at the whole … I have a tendency to look at everything at once. It seemed too big for me to tackle. So, they would say, "Practically, just find one thing. Whether it's write one email to your list, or create one landing page, or whatever practical thing that would be. Change your profile picture or whatever. Do one thing for your business that you can complete and check off a list to feel accomplished."

There is always a way to keep yourself plugged in. So, plug into a group, a Facebook group, or a mastermind group. Something where people are upbeat, positive, successful. Even if they're not successful monetarily, they're forging ahead. You're not in a depressive, woe is me, group. Find something that is motivating for you and inspiring for you. So, I did that.

Well, it took a while before I realized that it's going to have to take a lifestyle of that. It's not going to be: I'll do it one time, and then that will carry me for the rest of my life. It is a constant battle even today. Not today, but yesterday or a couple days ago, I was pretty down, feeling pretty unmotivated. I got on the phone with my current marketing consultant. She said, "I can tell right now, you're not into this." I said, "I'm not, I'm not. It's been too long since I've been really productive or felt really productive. I have business, but it's not exactly what I want, where exactly I want it. I haven't really produced as much as I want to."

Even though you're making money, or you have clients, or you have work to do, you can still fall back into that, "I'm still not living up to my own expectations" depression. We just sat on the call and worked on my mindset. Sometimes, you have to do that.

Another thing I found that I need to do is that I need to unplug completely. When you own your own business, you're really on call a lot of the time. Especially when you have those clients that have those immediate needs, you want to be on call. Getting yourself a business model where you can unplug for a period of time is vital to your sanity.

But it's hard and very demanding for people who are in the coaching industry, or the training industry. I don't think you can be in this business and succeed if you don't have a heart to help people. So, I know we want to help and you want to give of yourself, but if you're not refilling and revitalizing yourself, you're going to run out of steam.

I guess that's where depression can absolutely set in. You start burning out. You have those little tell-tell signs that you know about. You snap at somebody or you're not taking calls, or you're letting your work slip, or the quality is not as good. Those little things, you need to know what those are within yourself, so you can check that. keeping yourself up because no one is going to hold your hand. No one is going to come pick you up and take you to work. No one is going to do that for you—it's you.

I'm in some mastermind groups and some Facebook groups with some very highfalutin million-dollar company leaders. They talk about the times they were depressed. This isn't just because you make a million dollars, you're never going to be depressed or you're never going to be down on yourself. Anyone is susceptible to it.

TIPS FOR OTHER ENTREPRENEURS

You're not in isolation—know that you're not alone. Plug into a source that is going to help you. But, you have to go to it. No one is going to call you up and check on you every day. That is going to be a very rare thing, where people are going to check up on you everyday. If you fall into those mindsets, those negative mindsets, or those triggers, you know that you're getting kind of to the end or getting burned out, you need to go seek out help.

I guess some of us just want to sit back and have someone say, "What's the matter?" People aren't going to do that, so you need to go seek that out and make it a lifestyle. Add it to your to-do list during the day. Check in, or listen to this, or something else that inspires you. Make it a part of your daily routine and stock up.

Don't think that just because you're riding high this week or next week, that you're not going to come down, or you're not going to be depressed, sad, or discouraged. Keep feeding yourself, and as I said, kind of stock up so that when those times come, you know how it feels to be up. You can go seek that out, get that for yourself, and keep going.

I have push notifications on my phone—mine is scripture. You can also set that up for affirmations, prayers—whatever is going to help you. We all have our device; just make that the first thing you say each morning.

Also, I spoke to someone the other day, and he writes his affirmations in the shower with a dry-erase marker or something where he's just writing affirmations and things that he's thinking; his positive to-do's. Speaking life into yourself—it's got to happen everyday. Don't wait until you're down.

Gerri Milligan is passionate about health and wellness. She's in leadership at Mary Kay Cosmetics, and is a professional networker and holds the title of Executive Director of WOAMTEC (Women On A Mission To Earn Commission) Sugar Land Chapter. A professional women's networking group.

With several streams of income, you'll hear her say, "The sacrifice and struggle of starting businesses and making them profitable was worth it for me, so I could be home with my kids."

IF YOU DO THIS IT WILL HAPPEN.....NOT
BY KIM THORTON

MY STORY

Well, it's really a lot of things. When I first started out, I was very eager and excited. I thought, "Hey, if you do this, this will happen. If you do that, that will happen." I started when my kids were young. The only thing I knew about the Internet was barely how to find my email. I mean, when I was starting out, this wasn't really a huge thing that everyone had. Then, I took a few courses and learned how to build a website. All of this was incredibly daunting, because I had this one vision. I just wanted to write. The creative part, boom, I had that down. Not a big deal.

The technical part— and I didn't have the money to pay anybody — I had to learn. Well, like I said, I went from, "I think this is how I get my email," to, "Hey, I've got to build a website and now I've got to do this. Now, I've got to do the marketing, and now I've got to do this." The beginning stages took a long time just because it was so overwhelming and so daunting. My vision was incredibly large. I didn't necessarily have a funnel to work with. I worked with different coaches on different things, but the process alone wasn't getting me the results.

Well, obviously, I want everyone who I know could benefit from it to have my product. In order to make that happen, I had to do all these things. Well, I mean, literally, I was sitting at the computer crying, trying to figure out what possessed me to do this in the first place, because I really wanted to continue to do this. So, I continued to work towards it. But, sometimes you reach those crossroads. I said, "No. I have this vision. Let's go at it again." I continued to slowly chip away at it. Still, I wasn't getting the results that I wanted.

Even after years, I still wasn't getting the results that I wanted. I was in tears because I had invested time, money, effort, and energy. I was an expert. I could build you a website. I could create whatever you wanted. I would think that I should be a CEO at that point. I'd learned a lot, but I still wasn't where I wanted to be. So, I finally would conquer whatever challenge was in front of me, and then the rules of the game would change.

How do you market? How do you this? How do you do that? Literally, you spend money on trying to figure out how to do it, and then it changes.

It's enough to make you want to throw the computer out the window. I said to myself, "I'm just going to live off the grid and I'm going to eat locusts because this seems so much easier."

> **You have to keep growing.**

FINDING MY WAY OUT

My entire life everybody said to me, "You've always had this great gift." And, I've always used it in some capacity to bring joy and be creative. Why not be able to get paid for it? Not just because I'm in it to make money, but I can certainly go farther if I'm going to do that.

Well, the only way you can really get through it, and the way I did, is I took baby steps. What I began to see was not only that was I taking these steps, but I was conquering them. Someone had told me a long time ago, "Always celebrate your victories," because when you do that and keep a journal (and I'm not a journal person just stories) So, I started doing that. It really helped keep the vision in front of me. I was obsessed trying to figure this out."

My gosh. I created a website. Me, the same person who couldn't even figure how to get to her email created a website, and it was actually functional. That's huge. Then, I became an Amazon number one best-seller. Hello. That's huge. Then, it was all these other things. I built an email list. I've built a following on social media. Sometimes, you almost feel like the crickets are chirping, but when you look back, you're not where you want to be, but you see where you came from and it's just this incredible journey. Number one is definitely keeping in the vision before you, but number two, you have to always be learning.

You have to keep growing-even yourself. You just go in with, "I'm going to learn this. Learn the technical stuff," and everything's going to be hunky-dory. It is something within yourself that has to change. You have to always try to keep up with the next thing. As daunting as it is, as much as I sometimes wanted to throw the computer out the window, as much as I said, living off the grid and eating locusts was very, very plausible compared to even wanting to do this.

It's something inside of me a seed that was planted my entire life. People would say, "You've got this gift. Why aren't you doing this? I love what you do." I heard that over and over and it took years to accept that, because I never really had that much confidence in myself. The more I immersed myself into all of this—and I've stayed home so I could raise my children—it worked because I basically just got to work.

What gave me the confidence to do it was my relationship with God. That's very important to me, my faith. So, as I immersed myself and truly believed according to His word and I have seen miracles and I have seen Him show me wisdom and everything, it gave me the strength, the courage, and the ability to keep going.

Then within myself, what did I need to adjust? What did I need to change? How did I need to make this work better? What did that consist of? How do I fit this into my life? How did my life fit into this?

I don't know. For me, it became an obsession. Normally, I'm the type of person who doesn't have focus or goals. What really helped me in my journey, in life, was my faith and self-growing. I took seminars and I read books. Whatever it took to change my mind, my thinking, that's really I guess what did it for me.

TIPS FOR OTHER ENTREPRENEURS

Don't go into it with the mindset of "get-rich-quick". Anybody who promises you that you could get rich ... and even if you do get rich quick, things can change. You have relied on this formula or this opportunity or whatever to be "the thing" that's going to make you the money or your goal. If you're going into this, make sure that you have an idea of what you want to get out of it and that you're going to stick this out for the long haul. Be willing to bend and break, and become a completely different person if you have to be in order to achieve your goal.

That doesn't mean that you are somebody that no one recognizes, but what I'm saying is, the more you grow the more you become an expert at something. You really are a champion. So, that would be one thing. Just make sure you know that when you're getting into this that you're into this for the long haul. Then number two; always, always, always look at seminars or books or whatever it takes for you to grow as a person-whoever you see yourself as. Why would people even want to buy from you? There's got to be a reason. There's got to be a point.

Until you identify that for yourself, no one else is going to. Being who you are is really what's going to sell your product or services or whatever. So, always make sure that you are growing in the best possible way that you can. If you don't have the money to pay people ... I heard somebody say this to me one time, "You'll be surprised you actually have the money." You may not be able to go out to eat. You may have to go sell some things. You may have to do whatever self-sacrifice that you need to do in order to achieve that goal.

If it means that much to you, you will go find a way to make the money, to get that program or to purchase software-whatever it is that you need. So, always make sure that there's some type of sacrifice if that's what you need to do. I personally would say learn as much as technology or anything for yourself because you will save a lot of money that way. And yes it is frustrating, and yes you want to give up, but I have come such a long way. I'm very proud of that.

Remember, I went from, "Where's the email?" to creating websites and landing pages. I have an incredible following. I can do videos, create books and films, and whatever. It's been a really cool journey. I guess that's my tip. I did mine on a shoestring, you know?

That's why I tried to learn how to do all of this. So, it wouldn't break my family's bank. Even though the journey has been frustrating, it's also been gratifying. So, it's been worth that.

That was another thing. My husband knows a little more about HTML but when I was originally doing this, it got to a point where he couldn't help me. He was working full-time and trying to come home and do this. It was stressing him out. So, I really had no choice, but to learn.

If I really wanted to do this, I had to do it. Like I said it became a weird obsession for me, and I was just determined to make this a reality.

I think if I hadn't been trying to work on myself and my spiritual worth, none of that would've come or made a difference. I think it was because I knew that was still a possibility; it was very much within me. I could still accomplish this. I'm not as dumb as I think I am. And, as I'm going through that journey, it fuels my passion to be able to continue. Beyond that, if I hadn't had any kind of spiritual or self-growth, we would not be having this conversation.

Kim Thornton is a #1 Bestselling author of Christian children's books, an animation filmmaker, and a family blogger. She currently runs a Facebook Group for women in crisis.

RETHINKING MY LIFE
BY JILLIAN COLEMAN WHEELER

MY STORY

Depression has been a lifelong issue for me.

My background is as a psychotherapist and counselor. I first became interested in that field because as a young adult I suffered from unipolar depression. I was acutely depressed through my late teens and through my twenties, to the point where I was hospitalized at one point and was suicidal.

And gradually, through seeing a therapist and trying different medication approaches, and then getting my training as a therapist and working with clients while continuing to work on myself, I put together an approach to dealing with my own depression and helping clients deal with theirs that was effective.

By the time I was in my thirties, I had my depression under control. That's not to say that I didn't ever experience depression again, but I had integrated it into my life, so that I was able to manage my life effectively and have a career that worked. I was able to take good care of my children and have a functional life. But certainly, from time to time, depression has been an issue for me.

I was thinking of different times in my life, when depression has reared its ugly head and I've had to work through it again. Generally, that's been when circumstances in my life presented me with new kinds of challenges.

The one time that stands out for me is in 2009 and 2010. I think a lot of us working online, and people all over the world, remember that period as the near international depression, that economic recession that reached so many people in so many different work arenas. It certainly was devastating for many people who worked online.

By that time, I had stopped counseling and had begun working online, I was training grant writers. I was a consultant for non-profit agencies and private businesses. I was traveling around the country, speaking to investors, corporations, and companies that were interested in using particularly government grants to create affordable housing. I was working with clients and showing them how they could use government money to create affordable housing.

Also, I was training individual grant writers. I had a three-month training program. A lot of non-profits would send their beginning grant writers or grant writers who needed advanced training to me. A lot of people who wanted to learn how to get funding for projects that were near and dear to their hearts, and people who wanted to start non-profits in their communities, would enroll in my classes. These were fairly high-dollar classes.

My husband and I were working together in this business, and I was making a very comfortable mid-six-figure income in 2008. Then in 2009, when the whole industry sort of hit the skids and people stopped investing in non-essentials—and certainly in non-essential trainings—my income dropped from mid-six-figures to five-figures. It was a tremendous shock that affected everything in our lives.

For example, we had a home we had been living in for seven years. That was the year we had a balloon note, and we were due to refinance our home. Because our income had changed so radically, we were not able to qualify to refinance our home. Fortunately, we didn't have to face foreclosure. We were able to sell the house, but we did lose a lot of our equity.

And, the next year, 2010, one of my closest friends died of cancer. I took care of her while she was in hospice. And, it was really a time of rethinking my whole life. Our kids were all grown up and the younger ones were off on their way to college. It was time for me to really come to terms with what I wanted to do with the rest of my life.

I did deal with quite a bit of depression while I was going through that. So, I had to pull out my toolkit and start to figure out how to make it through that period of time.

> ❝ I think it's really important to acknowledge depression. ❞

FINDING MY WAY OUT

I almost stopped working for a couple of years, because my business pretty much tanked. I continued to sell a few classes, and so forth. But, a lot of the investors groups around the country stopped meeting because people were no longer investing in expensive properties. And so, a lot of things I had been doing to make money just stopped.

I was pretty depressed.

There's an expression that I use sometimes in working with my clients, when we're talking about having peace of mind. One of the things that make you feel good in life is having enough "Vitamin M"—and that's Money. Money is a source of a lot of our feelings of security, our feeling of having power in the world, and a lot of our feelings of hopefulness about the future come from not having it.

And, even though we know that money comes and goes, and it's really something we're able to manifest and create, and it has highs and lows…it's easier to feel good when we have it on hand. And, it's certainly easier to feel depressed when we don't have money. So, I did go through a lot of depression during that period; it was a challenge for me. I had to pull out a lot of the techniques that I've used in my life to deal with depression. And for me, those techniques are the same techniques that I use with my clients, the same techniques that gradually drew me out of the deep depression I was in when I was younger.

When I face depression, if I find myself falling into the pit of depression over anything, I find that the sooner I start using those techniques, the sooner I'm able to get level again and start functioning—and functioning much better.

For me, that is to acknowledge that I am probably depressed. And, often I don't notice that it's happening. Sometimes, my kids will notice or my husband will notice. And, one of them will say, "Have you taken your tryptophan in the last couple of days?"

I have a nutritional regimen that I do: taking supplements that I have found through trial and error are the right nutritional supplements for me.

I stop pushing myself and trying to accomplish things.

I generally rest and go to bed, and do only what I absolutely must do until I get through that period.

I return to my practice of meditation and make sure I'm meditating three or four times a day.

I get out in nature and walk near the water or walk through the forest and make sure that I'm actually walking for half an hour or an hour a day.

I do yoga.

I find if I do those things, and I allow myself to move through it until I start feeling better then I begin to get new ideas. I begin to gradually have energy. And a big part of that for me was realizing that I had been doing work that was lucrative and that I certainly felt good about what I was putting out in the world, but it was no longer the work that I really had a desire to do. And, maybe in that sense the Universe was supporting me in moving forward to the next thing.

It took me a few years to wend my way through the transition. That is how I gradually transitioned to the work that I'm doing now, which is closer to my counseling roots. I'm moving to working with people doing mentoring, to continue to speak, but speaking to organizations and groups about personal development issues, about depression and also about issues related to human potential and personal growth.

TIPS FOR OTHER ENTREPRENEURS

First of all, I think it's really important to acknowledge depression.

Carve out the space to nurture yourself through depression. Often people keep pushing themselves. And sometimes, you feel that you really have to do that. But, it's important to claim that space, to say, "I am in pain. I am unable to really move forward until I nurture myself to a better feeling place."

And, sometimes that means communicating to your spouse, to your children, to people you work with, just saying, "I'm not where I want to be right now, and I'm not always going to be this down, but right now, I just feel really bad…and I'm going to have to take a little time to get through this and help myself feel better."

Being holistic in my approach to life, I really believe that dealing with depression involves a holistic approach—that is a mental, physical and spiritual approach. Mental would be in the sense that some people need to be taking anti-depressants. I'm not a big fan of anti-depressants over the long term. But, some people who are deeply depressed, and particularly if you're feeling suicidal, then I think it's important to see a therapist, talk to a doctor, and to get the help you need in the interim. For a period of time, get the help you need to get out of feeling suicidal. And then, you can work on gradually finding nutritional supplements. They can take the place of anti-depressants.

I also think it's important to find a physical exercise regimen.

I do a course for my clients. It's called, *Reboot Your Bliss™, Help for Depression.* In that course, I encourage people to just start with a few minutes a day of walking outside, maybe just into your backyard or out in a park. Get out in nature and breathe. Just start with maybe ten minutes of walking and moving and having that physical experience of being in nature. So often, particularly people who are working a lot, we just completely cut ourselves off from nature. And nature is a big healing element.

If you type "hiking trails" into Google maps, you'll be surprised at what you'll find everywhere. If you're in a city, sometimes you just need to go to a neighborhood park. All cities have parks. Just start small. And, if you're too depressed to take more than five or ten minutes, then just go sit under a tree in a park, and walk around the tree for five minutes.

As you gradually increase your level of endorphins through the exposure that you have to nature, you'll find yourself increasing the energy you have and you'll find yourself being drawn to making more opportunities to be in nature. It's quite addictive being in nature. It's quite healing. And, the more you do it, the more you find yourself healing and the more you find yourself reaching out to find those opportunities to be in nature.

It's also important to be very patient with yourself. Give yourself the time you need. Recognize that if you had pneumonia, you wouldn't be expecting yourself to just get up and get over it immediately. If you had a really bad flu, you wouldn't expect yourself to just immediately get over it. So, it's important to be able to just give yourself the time you need to heal. And then gradually, start reaching out for what feels good.

Jillian Coleman Wheeler is a consultant, speaker, mentor and creator of Reboot Your Bliss™. She works with individuals and organizations. Jillian offers classes, speaking and writing about personal development, depression, mental health and success in life and work. She is the co-author of five books, and her book on overcoming depression will be published in the coming months.

ALCOHOL, DEPRESSION, & FAITH
BY WILLIE CRAWFORD

MY STORY

My story was one of alcoholism. I went into the military and they put me in very dangerous situations. I'd land the airplane and I needed alcohol to calm me down because I was scared. Alcohol's a very strong depressant, stronger than most other addictions, drugs. That was what pushed me into the corner and what pulled me out of that was the military sending me to a rehab program. I went to it and they said, "You need to keep your nose clean for two years, so you can retire and get your retirement pay." I did that and yet I know now that a big part of that was accepting too many projects, too much responsibility.

Each individual person can only do so much and so I took on so much that at times I felt overwhelmed. I think that's what pushed me over the edge. I guess I was depressed, but at times I just didn't know what to do. I pulled out of it. I don't want people to think that you need to be perfect. Life is what it is. You face these challenges.

> **I believe that things will work out the way they're supposed to and so I don't fear anything**

FINDING MY WAY OUT

I went through a rehabilitation program where they introduced me to Alcoholic Anonymous. They don't like you talking about the program too much because if you talk about the program too much and you slip, you drop off, then it's not a very positive thing for them. That's what turned me around. It was seeing there was hope out there. That was the biggest thing.

I went though seven wars. Some of them were called conflicts other's were called wars. People pointed missiles and anti-aircraft artillery at my airplane. That scared the living daylights out of me. Yeah. I had to pretend not to be afraid. I'd land and to calm my nerves, I'd have a drink. But also, I grew up very poor and there's a part of me that feared going back to where I came from. I reached for very big goals. Right now, I'm launching a TV show. That's how big I reach, but there is a fear of going back to where you came from.

It scares me a little and Alcoholics Anonymous have a saying, "A problem shared is a problem cut in half." The greatest thing you can do is to reach out to somebody else who cares about you and your loved ones, your family members, your children, your spouses, whoever, coworkers, they care about you. You have to acknowledge, "I can't pull out of this on my own. I need help." Once you reach out for help, they will help you.

My boss drove me to rehabilitation and he said, "We're here for you." He said, "Get yourself together." Your loved ones, people who care about you, are there for you, but you've got to ask for help. I'm trying to remember what verse in the Bible.... what did it say? "Ask and you shall receive. Knock and the door shall be open unto you," and a bunch of other things, but it's basically ask for help. If you don't ask for help, then you're not letting people know that you need the help.

It is very significant that we, at times, need help. If you don't let people who care about you know that you need help, how are they going to know that maybe you were just asking them to extend a hand? They can pull you out of a depression, or a suicidal mood, or whatever. I went through a very deep depression one time where I drove around with a loaded .44 Magnum in my car, a handgun, and I thought, "Okay, I can't stop drinking. It's an addiction," and I sat on the edge of a pond one day with a loaded gun, and I cupped it, and put it next to my head. I thought, "I want somebody to be here with me and feel sorry for me." I'm like, "That's the craziest thing ever," but I wanted somebody to feel sorry for me, to hold me. I've been through that.

I've been through depression. I've been through suicidal moods. I've been through all kinds of things, and I have friends who are billionaires. Bill Bartmann, the first time I saw him, he said, "You know a billion is a thousand million?"

I'm like, "Okay?" I thought, "I want to be a billionaire." I still do. I'm not, of course, but I have very ambitious goals. I want to do good for the world. I dislike cancer and I've lost so many friends to it that that depresses me at times. I lost my grandmother. I lost a bunch of friends to that.

So, I've had much success in my business and being successful in business is not a straight line up. No. No. No. No. No, no, no. The IRS sent me a bill for $160,000 and they said, "You didn't file the proper paperwork for these years, and so we figure you owe us $160,000." I called the young lady. I won't say what I said, but she said, "You're one of us. You said you're a government worker and you know you need to file the proper paperwork." She said, "Just file the paperwork and the bill will probably go away."

I got a bill for $160,000 and I'm like, "Gosh." I won't even say what I thought, but it's like, "You can't be serious." I'm a Christian and I believe in a higher power. I believe that things will work out the way they're supposed to, so I don't fear anything, but it's like when somebody says, "Oh, you owe us $160,000." It's like, "Are you kidding me?"

I knew that it will work out, but it's still a little intimidating.

TIPS FOR OTHER ENTREPRENEURS

The main tip that I would tell other people is having faith, having hope, and reaching out. I have faith and I don't believe that my faith needs to be their faith. I've been around so many people who, they'll say, "Well, you know, this and that?" No. No. This is my belief, you know? I believe in a higher power. I believe in a God, and I believe in Jesus, and Mary, and all that Christianity stuff. And that's part of it, to believe that it's all going to work out the way it's supposed to.

The other thing is I have a friend, Jim Straw, who made $550 million before he passed away maybe three years ago. Jim said, "You just do something. You can't just sit there and wait for the problem to solve itself." That is probably one of the most important tips he gave me, do something. If you don't do something, the problem's not going to solve itself. It will not solve itself. You might do the wrong thing, but that'll tell you did a wrong thing, and you can go back, and fix it.

I believe that I'm only going to go around once that I know of. I don't need to be afraid to take risks to do what I feel I'm meant to do, but depression is very strong. Life is good, but it's what you make of it. You cannot be afraid to take chances, but not foolish risk.

Willie is one of the world's leading Internet marketing experts. He has written three physical books and over 70 e-Books, published a newsletter nonstop, spoken at over 100 live seminars, five of which he's hosted, hosted over 500 podcasts on online radio shows, created over 150 information products, and mentored several thousand students, some of whom are very successful. He has been doing this since 1996. He stepped out of uniform in the Armed Forces after a 20-year career; he has never needed to work for anyone else and truly lives the laptop lifestyle.

WHAT'S WRONG WITH ME?
BY BETSY M. HALL

MY STORY

I have worked in sales for ten years. I love sales. A few years ago, I took a part-time position with a non-profit, stepping back into administrative work. Working more as a manager required different ways of thinking than sales. One day, they switched me out of that position into development. I was being asked to switch right back into sales at half the pay.

It was a hard switch making that mindset and skill switch back to being more in sales and asking for donations. I had dedicated myself to excellence, so I really got stuck on why I got transferred to this other position. I asked myself, "What is wrong with me?" I couldn't get an answer for that, and it really was debilitating.

I was frozen. I didn't know how to approach the next position. I would have done better if I had had more support. Instead of being able to be creative and say, "Well, I don't have these resources, so what can I do next?" I spent a lot of my brain power asking that question, "What's wrong with me? What's wrong with me?"

I was just talking with an entrepreneur about entrepreneurs and depression and he was going through the same thing. He was asking himself, "What's wrong with me?"

❝ Don't be so hard on yourself. ❞

FINDING MY WAY OUT

The non-profit where I had worked part-time and I decided to part ways, and then I was able to get back into focusing on my own business. I was able to work with people who could come alongside me, get the information I needed, and get me the resources I needed, plus be supportive. I actually now have more business than I can keep up with.

I can't pinpoint what gave me the courage to change and leave my position, It's the same thing as the previous position I had left when I was selling newspaper ads; it was just not working, and I knew that I could make more money, and be more profitable for the people I was working with by being able to expand what I was offering. Instead of just offering the newspaper ad, I could offer multiple ways of doing marketing and that would be more effective for my clients while staying in integrity with who I was. When I'm in a position where I'm asked to not be in integrity with who I am and what I feel led to do, then I just move on.

TIPS FOR OTHER ENTREPRENEURS

Just relax. Don't be so hard on yourself. "Nobody likes a bully," as sales expert Eric Lofholm says. "Don't beat yourself up." "Results take as long as they take." Those are all "Eric Lofholmisms". Listen to encouraging professionals. There are plenty of low-cost and no-cost resources to tune into when you need some encouragement and you need to get a shot in the arm.

Here are some examples: I would substitute that unsupportive question, "What's wrong with me?" to sometimes ask, "What is right with me? What are my strengths?" You may have to ask other people for that because it's hard to be objective. I think for me personally, it's hard to be objective. And then, just focus on what resources are around you. What can be your next step that's going in the direction that you want to go? And then, pat yourself on the back for taking those steps, and acknowledge the progress that you've made. Have a partner or a group to celebrate with. Ellen Violette and I facilitate masterminds together and one of our focus points every week is to celebrate the accomplishments of each and every member.

So I say, celebrate what you've been able to do. That gives you some perspective instead of always focusing on what's undone and what's not done up to your standards. And then, just know that the resources are at hand. It may be a person. It may be an idea. It may be a different way of doing something. It will be provided for you, and it will take you to the next step of where you're going.

One place to find resources is networking events. I just went to a networking event, and there were a lot of other people who are entrepreneurs, solopreneurs and salespeople there. I know it can be scary if you don't know anyone, and yet most people are in the same boat. So, I just consider myself the hostess of the event even though I'm usually not the one who has organized it. I just show up; it's my entrepreneurial job to introduce people, to welcome people. I've even been asked, "Are you the organizer?"

"No, I'm just showing up."

I would also say accept yourself. If you're going to have a moment of depression, just let yourself have it. If you're going to have a crisis, let yourself have that crisis. Give yourself ten minutes or whatever it is to have it, and then beyond that remunerating and going over it, and announcing it and whatever, then go to the next step and say, "Okay, I've had my moment."

From 10:00 to 10:15, I'm allowed to scream, yell, run around, pray, get upset, whatever it is. And then say, "Okay, even though that problem still exists, I'm not going to live in that. I'm going to do something. I'm going to take some action."

Betsy M. Hall makes connections. She connects associates, partners, clients, and friends. She also connects people with marketing tools that complement each other. She communicates messages to individuals in the marketplace through scripting, graphic design, phones, emails, texts, web ads, print ads, printed materials, emails, blogs, social media and more. She loves coming from the heart.

She offers marketing directions to entrepreneurs like Realtors and health professionals who just want to do what they love. She also leads workshops and masterminds, providing creative people with support for business/personal/spiritual expansion and task completion.

SUCCESS IS A TEAM SPORT
BY RICK COOPER

MY STORY

Every year in my business, I have faced some type of challenge that was beyond my control, and I had to adapt. It's like the example of an airplane flying from New York to Los Angeles. The airplane spends about 80% of the trip off course. So, how can it possibly arrive on time at the right airport? The answer is course correction. They are constantly making adjustments to get back on track. So, I'll share two of the biggest challenges I have gone through with you.

The first was when my father passed away in 2016. His death was unexpected. I loved my dad and felt a lot of regrets after I lost him. The last few months of his life were complete turmoil, and it turned my life upside down. Plus, after he died, it impacted my business. I felt a lot of grief and didn't really feel like myself. It was a daily struggle for six months before I felt like I was getting back to normal.

And, I have had many times over the years when I was coaching clients that I heard stories about people going through a death in the family, a divorce or a health crisis that shut down their ability to work. Now, I know what that feels like.

It's easy to underestimate how our circumstances affect our attitude and mindset. You have to stay focused and deliberate if you want to build a successful business.

Also, focus on the basics: eat well, sleep, spend time with people you love, and practice gratitude.

> ❝ I try to just trust in God and recognize the opportunities that come my way. ❞

FINDING MY WAY OUT

For the second big challenge, I'll backtrack a moment to four years prior. I began attending church. I first went to church because they were hosting "Financial Peace University" led by Dave Ramsey. They had trained facilitators; they played a DVD from Dave each week, and then had a group discussion. I loved it and ended up attending twice.

Somewhere along the way, I came to Christ. I started attending church because I realized I needed to work not only on my finances, but also my spirituality. I always considered myself a Christian, but never formally asked Jesus into my heart and got baptized.

So, at the age of 38, I was baptized. I can remember the day clearly. It was a warm day in May. They had a large metal tub out on the lawn. I stood in it and was baptized. The pastor dunked me in the tub—full immersion. And, the first thing I saw when I came up was a bunch of small children dancing around in front of me. I thought I was in heaven and the cherubs had gathered round. I can still see the joyful expression on their faces.

My faith has become very important to me over the years. And, I recognize when God is working in my life.

Here's an example of one of God's blessings, which was the second big challenge. I had a conversation with my mentor, Eric Lofholm, who is a master sales trainer, where he asked me to team up with him. He said, "Times are tough. You have skills I need, and I have a structure and team that you could benefit from working with. Let's work together."

And, of course, I said, "Yes".

I always imagined that I would be independent in business. I could do everything on my own. I didn't need other people. They say success is a team sport, and now I believe that. You will do better when you work as part of a team. Whether you are the leader or a follower, you will benefit from collaborating with others.

While all of this was happening, I was having a crisis of confidence. Before I went to work with Eric, I was facing all sorts of challenges. Every day, I woke up with a sense of urgency that I had to make something happen. It was very stressful. I had a knot in my stomach. My body ached from the stress. I wasn't taking good care of myself. I wasn't sleeping well. And, it was creating challenges in my personal relationships.

But, I focused on the things in my business that would produce results. I was getting better day-by-day, but the challenging economy made it difficult to get results.

I have to thank Eric for stepping in when he did with that opportunity.

When something good shows up in your life you have to recognize it and take advantage of it.

It's like the story of the man in the flood, standing on his roof waiting for God to save him. A boat comes by, then a helicopter, and the man waves them off saying he was waiting for God to save him. He ends up drowning, and then goes to heaven. He confronts God and asks him why he didn't save the man. He was faithful to God and believed that God would save him. Then, God says, in calming tones, I tried to save you. I sent a boat, and then I sent a helicopter. End of story.

We often don't like how God shows up in our life. It is not according to our own plan. I try to trust in God and recognize the opportunities that come my way. In fact, I coauthored a book, titled *Seize Your Opportunities* with several amazing authors. It's very inspiring.

Eric Lofholm says, "Change begins in language." You need to change the way you look at yourself and how you communicate with yourself. For example, you can use positive affirmations to change your beliefs.

TIPS FOR OTHER ENTREPRENEURS

Many of my clients are coaches, speakers, trainers and consultants. They are people who have a message they want to share with the world. I help them attract clients online.

Here are three simple tips to help you take action and move forward:

1. Gratitude
I think a good place for anyone to start is with gratitude. I journal every day for about 10-15 minutes. As part of that journaling, I make a list of three things I am grateful for. I have

to think about the good things in my life—the things, people, and opportunities that I appreciate.

Remember that the practice of gratitude can help you overcome sadness and depression. It helps to shift your focus away from your challenges and toward your blessings.

2. Daily Plan of Action
You can work on your mindset, but that is not going to be enough to move you forward. You can learn and improve your skills, but that is still not enough to produce results.

You actually have to take action.

And that's a challenge for people who are struggling. For someone who is having a crisis of confidence, they just want to go back to bed and hide under the covers. That's not going to cut it. At a certain point, you have to take personal responsibility and get into action.

When I am coaching business owners, I have to evaluate their mindset and make sure we work on increasing their confidence and getting them into action.

So, my tip is to create a daily plan of action. There is a specific technique that I learned many years ago called the Success Six. It's a technique that Ivy Lee taught Charles Schwab, President of Bethlehem Steel in the early 1900's.

Here's how it works. Sit down the night before or early in the day and make a list of your top six tasks or priorities for the day. Next, order the tasks from one through six. Then, start on the first task and work it through to completion. Then, move on the next task, and so on, until you complete all six tasks.

This takes the guesswork out of the day. And when you are emotional and stressed, it is tough to make decisions. So, having a short list of six tasks will help you have a great day and feel better about things.

In *Seize Your Opportunities*, I said, "You lose focus when you are distracted. So, it's important to reduce interruptions and distractions. Keep coming back to your goals and priorities. Acknowledge that in any given moment, you have a choice of what to work on. So, make a choice to work on tasks that will give you the best results."

This is not always easy to do when you are feeling depressed. But, it's important to try to accomplish it.

3. Focus on Your Core Gifts

It's easy to get overwhelmed, especially when you are trying to do work that is beyond your skill set. You can certainly learn how to do new things, but a better approach might be to focus on your core gifts and outsource the rest.

Look at it this way, you are much more likely to do work you love and find easy to do. Remember, that there are other people out there who are skilled in areas where you are weak.

It frees you up to focus on areas where you can add the most value. By doing this, you will spend more of your time on enjoyable work.

The other benefit is that you will spend more of your time in flow. Tapping into your flow state allows you to peak perform. It's that feeling you get when you are unstoppable.

And there's nothing to cure depression like getting on a lucky streak where everything seems to go your way.

So, start by identifying your core gifts. What are those skills that you have mastered? What could you do all day, easily and effortlessly?

And then identify one role that you can give up. Find one project you can delegate. And look for someone who will take it off your hands.

You will feel much more energized and refreshed when you know that someone else is working and getting things done without you having to do anything. That will save you time, energy and effort.

I think that if people follow these tips, they can get through it and have an impact on the world!

Rick Cooper, MBA is an online marketing and social-media trainer, author speaker, coach, and Wordpress website designer.

BACK INTO THE WORKFORCE, REALLY?
BY BROOKLYN REYES

MY STORY

I launched an online business, so this was my first time doing everything virtually. I spent a lot of time; I did all the right things, I took a lot of courses, which is how I got introduced to Ellen Violette.

I got really depressed that it took so much time to put together my website and my offerings.

When I got everything online, I expected to publish and have all these people just come to my website and buy my offerings without really doing much besides getting published.

I put myself out there on the web and thought that that was going to be enough. And, I was so excited. I launched the website, and I would tweet about it and use LinkedIn because LinkedIn is where I gravitated—I tend to be a little bit more business oriented, so that's where I went in social media. But, nobody was buying any of my offerings. I had put together two of my very first virtual products, which were the handbook and also coaching packages. And, it was crickets.

It was really depressing to be so excited and inspired to get so much done and nobody was coming. At the time, I was at my house. I had two little kids, and I wasn't putting myself out there very much. I just wanted to network with the people I already had connections with, and I thought it would take off from there. But, nothing happened. And I thought to myself, "How am I going to be successful?"

You have to go out and talk to people. You're building relationships when you're at work, so you have to take that same framework and apply it to your business.

I don't think one person even signed up for my quick free offering, and I didn't have any bites on my coaching packages, so that's where it started.

> **❝ Never lose that vision of what you really want. ❞**

FINDING MY WAY OUT

What changed was I actually went back to work. Now, I want to explain why that actually helped me. In my specific circumstance, it got me out there again, so I started to get back into the day-to-day hustle. I had been hanging out at home on my own schedule, so really just getting back and working, I felt like I was in the trenches again. I started to network and get back on my people skills.

I had been staying at home for about five years, so it really helped my confidence. Now I HAD to be there; I had a deadline. I had a team that I worked with. You can become really isolated when you work by yourself, especially when it's virtual from home. So, my confidence grew.

When I got back into day-to-day work, it was hard. But, that is really what got me out of depression. I did take some steps back as far as income from being at home. But, I was able to work my way back up very quickly, which gave me even more confidence. I saw that I was successful in this area, so why couldn't I be successful having this business on the side?

It gave me the confidence to get back out and try an online business again—the right way.

Now, I know nobody is going to just find me. I have to have a strategy. I have to add value.

And, I think what also helped was the thought that if I were going to write about how to reduce stress with work, and how to handle work better, shouldn't I be in that situation where I'm working? When you write about something, you have to be in it. And, that made this book much easier to write because I was actually doing it.

TIPS FOR OTHER ENTREPRENEURS

You have to get out of your house. I really believe you have to pound the pavement-whatever that looks like. For me, it was getting back into the workforce. Other people might do it other ways. I think that's the big key. Also, I never lost the vision of what I did want-even when I went back to work.

I look back at the goals I'd written. I look at blog posts I wrote, and I'm the same person. I still have the same goals. The core of what you want, or the core passions never really go away. They might have some variations. So, never lose that vision of what you really want. It just might manifest differently. I never thought in a million years I'd be back at work, but I am. And I never thought I would finish a book, but I am.

When I look at the goals I wrote down they were: I want to write a bestseller self-help book. If you would have told me two years ago, "Brooklyn, you wrote that." I would have said, "Oh my gosh I did; I can't believe I wrote that." And, if you asked me when I was 17 what I wanted…that was exactly what I would have said.

But, if you are working at home, go to Meetups. Go to conferences, absolutely. Sit down and talk to people. Learn what they want and provide value. That's what I've learned over the past couple of years. I look back at what I was offering before and I ask myself, "Was that really providing value?"

Well, how do you provide value? You have to know what people need. When I started working again was when I had that mentality shift. How can I provide value? Then you just expand on that. You use the same principles.

How can I serve the people I'm working with in a different way? So, just provide value, and I think you'll always be successful. I didn't have that mentality when I was doing business the first time. Maybe it was ego driven, I don't know, but this is my third business.

My first one was when I was 19, I tried to start feng-shui consulting, and I did the at-home thing three or four years ago. Then, my husband and I started a business. That's been hard. And now, I'm launching a book. This is try number four, so it definitely does not unfold as you think it would, and you really have to go along for the ride and align yourself with the right people.

Brooklyn Reyes is the author of The Stress Buster Handbook for Work & Life, 12 Strategies for Removing Negative Thinking, Living Beyond Fear and Creating a Happier Life. She studied psychology at the University of Utah, earning a master's degree in psychology focused on corporate culture. She coaches career-driven 9 to 5ers learn how to deal with stress in work and life.

WHAT THE MIND CAN BELIEVE, THE MIND CAN ACHIEVE
BY CHRISTEN VIOLETTE

MY STORY

After I got back from the Korean War, I went to work at Douglas Aircraft. Douglas had huge contracts with the Army, Navy, Air Force and NASA, and they built commercial airliners too. And, all the equipment had to be inventoried and put into computers.

I was a supervisor in plant management in charge of the inventory and computer crews. A Navy contract had been cancelled, and I went over with the inventory crew to that area. There was a man sitting in an office; he was 50 years old. He had been with Douglas Aircraft for 20 years. They put him in charge of that contract. And when the Navy contract got cancelled, he got cancelled along with it. He told me that he was buying a house, he had kids in college, and that Douglas wouldn't find another place for him in the company; he had tears in his eyes. So, I said to myself right then and there, "So much for job security and being a company man." That's when I knew I had to do something else.

So, I got my real estate license.

I was born and raised in Los Angeles, California. I grew up west of downtown and everything west of there was bean fields. And, I heard a lot of "would've", "could've", "should've" stories all my life about how this person could have bought a lot for $1000 and on and on. There were opportunities in an area called Antelope Valley, north of Los Angeles, and there was real potential. People could buy a 2½-acre parcel for cheap and set it aside, because there was a lot of growth potential out there, and there was a very good chance that it would be worth a lot of money one day.

So, I became a land consultant. Because of my upbringing, I believed in investing in land, and I did very well. But, it never seemed to be enough for me. I went into management because

I figured instead of just earning money, I could teach other people how to do it, and I would get an override off of their sales.

Next, I headed up a company, and then I went into business for myself with a partner. I moved to San Jose where he had an office already, and we started building from there. We actually got to a point where we had gorgeous offices all over California, one in San Francisco overlooking the bay, one in a new high-rise on Sunset Boulevard on the Strip. It took us a while to hire managers and teach them how to manage, recruit, and train. They recruited land consultants, and soon we had hundreds of land consultants and managers, and we had just turned the corner.

I have to tell you, at that time, land investment was very popular with a lot of real-estate companies, and I don't know why, but they were skirting the laws all over the place and getting caught. They were selling property out in the boonies. It was recreational property, and they were selling it as an investment. They would clear the land off and build a nice pavilion there. They would have people drive up to it and have a cookout, and then they would buy it. Years later, they would drive up there to see their investment and the weeds were higher than the pavilion, and they couldn't sell the property for what they paid for it, which resulted in class-action suits.

The Department of Real Estate was coming into our offices every week checking our files. We had everything signed; we did everything right. But, they were so fed up with land-investment companies that they decided they didn't want us there. So, they used a rule and regulation that they used against the recreation guys. They said we could no longer call legally subdivided land an investment. We couldn't use the word "speculation", and they sent us a cease and desist letter.

And, we were going, "My God, what's going on here?" So, we got an Antelope-Valley newspaper and took it to them to show them there were all these properties for sale, some of them very close to our parcels that were selling as investments.

They said, "Well, those properties aren't legally subdivided." Think about that. So we went to our attorney, and he said, "You can't fight these people; they have unlimited funds and the State." And if you beat them, they will appeal it back and forth, and you don't have the money to fight these guys.

They even had a guy at the San Francisco Examiner who smeared us in the newspaper. So, we ended up going bankrupt for about $500,000 a piece. We had been on our way to being millionaires, so that was a hard pill to swallow. We put a lot of time and effort into growing it. And, once it happened, I hit the floor. It was hard for me to pick myself up.

> **❝** Read success books, do self-hypnosis or deep meditation—whatever it takes! **❞**

FINDING MY WAY OUT

I read a lot of success books, and I read stories about how several people who became very successful had failed several times. And in addition to reading success stories, I read books on self-improvement.

In those days, there was *Psycho-Cybernetics* and *Think and Grow Rich*. One of the things that really affected me in *Think and Grow Rich* was the idea that what the mind can conceive and what the mind will believe, the mind can achieve. And, I followed that.

I studied self-hypnosis and found out that we carry a lot of misinformation in our subconscious minds that causes us to react negatively in life, and I figured the best way to reach the subconscious mind was to do self-hypnosis. I learned it, and I did it. It made me feel really good. I even used hypnosis to get myself into a deep meditative level and do mantras that were good. That helped me overcome what I was going through.

So, I used it to keep giving myself positive suggestions. When you are in a hypnotic state, you are very relaxed, and it calms you down.

Also, I had lived on less than what I made, so I had some money set aside to figure out what I'd do next. A friend of mine who was in real estate came to me and told me about this real-estate company that was suffering. It was having a really hard time because of all the franchise real-estate offices that were growing up, and he was having trouble recruiting more salesmen.

I looked at his business; it was old and tired and he didn't know what to do for an encore. I turned his whole business around, and he paid me very well for being a consultant. Then, that ended. But, in the meantime, it gave me confidence and made me feel good about myself again.

And since I was very interested in self-hypnosis, it wasn't that difficult to make my decision, which was to study it and become a certified hypnotherapist. I just seemed to have a knack for that. I made a very good living doing it until I retired.

TIPS FOR OTHER ENTREPRENEURS

My best tip is to get your mind straight. If your mind is straight—whether you do self-hypnosis or read self-improvement books and follow what they say, the most important thing is your mind—it can help you to come out of depression or from getting too depressed, so that's what I recommend.

Do whatever it takes to keep yourself motivated. Read success books, do self-hypnosis or deep meditation.

In the final analysis, you're the only one who can keep yourself motivated and moving forward.

And, never give up.

Christen Violette is a retired clinical hypnotherapist, former real-estate investor, audio-recording engineer and aerospace manager. He is also a Korean Vet with a purple heart. Christen is now writing a book on his process to help people understand what he has shared at a deeper level and to explain how far reaching our mind really is.

THE TRUTH SHALL SET YOU FREE
BY MARY LATELA

For decades, I hid family secrets inside of me.

It got to the point where I felt stuck in my business and my writing until I could reveal my embarrassing story.

When I got my Twitter account, found other writers, and some supportive places, I realized that I wasn't the only one who was in the middle of this kind of situation, and that I needed to start thinking about writing about this.

As a young woman, my father violated me…repeatedly, over time.

My mother knew, but would never tell.

I decided to put together a short essay about a typical night: my father coming in and doing his disgusting thing, and the next morning, my mother asking me if he had indeed slept with me. All I remember was nodding my head, her turning around and going about her business, and that was all.

She never did anything or said anything about it. Nothing to defend me. She didn't call up her brother and say, "Come on over here, your brother-in-law's gone mad" or something. I basically kept quiet about it, and they did too. There was never any support.

I have found that silence is not good for family secrets like this. I knew I had to speak the words. I have spoken hard things before, so I prepared myself, sort of , over the past summer to do that, because I felt that I was stuck and couldn't go any farther in my business. And, I just couldn't go any farther with my writing. I feel that honesty is absolutely necessary when you're in a helping profession, and keeping this big secret was a barrier for me. I knew I had more stories to tell-especially this, related to relationships.

Part of my preparation was asking myself, "Would I use my real name?" And I decided that of course I would use my real name. After my divorce, I changed my name, which helped a great deal. It was changed 20 years ago, but it was helpful now because my name is uniquely mine and no one can say I was talking about them.

Once this material came out on the Internet, in an Internet magazine, I received so many supportive messages from women. Some saying, "Wow, that is very brave of you. I don't know if I could ever tell a story like that." And others actually saying, "You know? Your story could be My Story." And, that was it.

I had been more or less inside myself, introverted, and feeling that these secrets were my fault. Then, I came to a very clear understanding that no, this is not my fault. I know that many women have been in abusive situations. They are blamed, and they just suck it up and take it. And, I realize that's not right. Of course, if my best friend came to me and told me this similar story, I would say, "Of course you're not to blame, this is a sickness, and you are the victim; you had no way to change it."

I had really been in a place where I was stuck. And, my hope was that deciding to actually be as honest as possible would help others.

What a relief and an encouragement it was when I shared My Story—not the entire saga—and people said either that they understood about secrets or have had a similar experience and maybe this would get them ready to talk about it.

The truth is that I have been struggling with depression for most of my adult life and had to go on and do the things that I have had to do: teach, take care of my children, and keep that buttoned up. I realized that stuffing the pain could make you sick.

I think the family secret aspect of it is: if your mother and father weren't there for you as your mother or father, you more or less have to come to some point where you realize, "Mom and Dad, you are not my mom and dad. You didn't do the things that moms and dads are supposed to do, which is to protect their children. Therefore, I'm not going to have anything to do with you. I separated myself from them for quite some time.

We never came to a full understanding. And now, they both have passed away. There wasn't a resolution or apology of any kind at all. But, I think that's true of someone who has been really abusive. In order to apologize for that, they would have to apologize for 20-million things, and it's just not possible. I've come to understand that and that I'm not in danger now. I do have to be very careful both in my personal life and in my professional life not to get caught up in the kinds of manipulation that are behind many family secrets.

So, when I'm working with somebody who asked me to help them with a resume or something off the beaten path, it's kind of a similar story. They'll say to me, "Well you know, I don't have a typewriter, you'll have to type it for me." It may seem like a minor issue, but this depresses me.

I explain that I'm not going to type it for them. I tell them, "You'll have to go to the library where they have computers and sit down to do this.." I don't take on others' responsibilities. I consider their asking me to do their work as passive-aggressive behavior, and it's manipulative. It's almost like some people are kind of addicted to having everybody do everything for them, and they can spot a kind person a mile away. I am a kind person; I help people and they know that.

Self-care is also important. I have a yoga program that I do three times a week. I also read for fun. I have a really nice group of friends on Twitter and also out in the world. When they write a book, I read it and usually review it, and it's a lot of fun. When you're doing all the right things and you're depressed—well, that seems just terrible. When you are actually doing something productive, you help yourself and help others too. I think the best way to deal with depression is to be active in areas that you really enjoy.

> **❝ You have to take care of yourself, and you have to have 'me time'. ❞**

TIPS FOR OTHER ENTREPRENEURS

You have to take care of yourself, and you have to have "me time"… and I don't mean every two years you go to a spa. I mean everyday taking care. There's a lot of rich material around self-care and people to help you. I have been happy to work with some teachers in mindfulness, in yoga, in some of the other practices… they are called "new age", but they are really ancient acupuncture/acupressure practices. These are things that we can do for ourselves.

Also, don't be afraid to take a nap. I know many people who will do anything they can to get away from the idea of taking a nap.

Others of us who say, a half-hour nap in the afternoon means that when I wake up I'm starting the second part of my day. In other words, I take care of myself, and if I'm sick, for goodness' sake, I stay home. I go to the doctor; I have the checkups that one should have. Women in my mother's generation were trained to only do things for everybody else—even if it wears you to death.

And, what do you do when you have no home, no money, no nothing? You find things to do. You volunteer. You go out and do something that's meaningful, or even not so meaningful, but something so that you interact with people.

I had one time in my life when I was alone, going through this divorce and didn't have a job. I decided I would go over to the Red Cross; they never say no to volunteers, they always give you coffee, and treat you so nicely because they run on volunteers. This led to a full-time job with them and got me back into going on from there to finishing my graduate work for the final attempt. So, if you have to, get a job.

I gave myself time to go inside. In facing the pain and disappointment, I relieved myself of feeling shame and guilt. And then, I turned outward. As a volunteer, an employee, an entrepreneur and a writer, I serve others and help them to heal. In bringing my dark places to the light, I have found acceptance and encouragement. My depression decreases as my feeling of isolation decreases and my feeling of value increases. In caring for myself, I am more able to care for others.

Mary Latela, M.Div. (Yale), is an educator, pastoral counselor, and author focusing on self-empowerment, and healing for persons dealing with physical, mental, and emotional issues, for caregivers and survivors of abuse and violence. "By dealing with my own experiences, moving beyond simply surviving, I have learned to reach out and connect with others by empathic listening, reflection, and conversation." Mary is the author of 15 published creative non-fiction books

TALKING TO AN ANGEL
BY JOY PEDERSON

MY STORY

There were a couple of incidents that occurred where I noticed that I wasn't feeling or doing my best. I didn't necessarily equate it to depression at the time, but once you get out of it, you realize it is a form of depression.

In my case, when I wrote my first book, *Wisdom of the Guardian: Treasures from Archangel Michael to Change Your Life*, which Archangel Michael actually asked me to write , I didn't want to tell anyone about it. But, because I had been channeling for many years, I wrote it effortlessly.

Channeling is a way of receiving information from outside of yourself. It's a form of telecommunication, but without any equipment. So, I actually receive the information from another being. Then, I use a form of channeling called "Automatic Writing" and I am able to either write or type the information, which comes through me telepathically as I am a "Vessel"

The challenge wasn't the writing part; I had issues about telling people that I communicate with angels because I worked in the business community. What I realized was that it was fear, and the fear depressed me. It caused me not to want to go out and do what I needed to do to have the information reach people.

> Stop the self-limiting talk.

FINDING MY WAY OUT

So, I figured I needed to do a healing on myself regarding what was blocking me from doing what was necessary to share the information with others. I used a form of spiritual healing on myself that I had been doing for years on other areas of my life.

Because I could also remember past lives, I tuned into my past lives discovering many lifetimes where I was persecuted in one way or another. As I recalled those memories of persecution, such as being maimed, murdered, hanged, beheaded, and burned at the stake, I cleared those memories and the emotional attachments to them. These were all things of the past experiences that I did not want to repeat. Those memories were creating blocks to my being fully self-expressed.

Each time I cleared those types of negative memories and emotions, the more I found my voice and was able to speak more confidently and effectively regarding my ability to channel angels and the specific work that I was doing with Michael. Then, I was able to get the book published and speak about the book publicly to promote it.

The subconscious is our memory bank and computer. It is the part of us that manifests and projects out, attracting our results. It can play back memories of events that didn't go well, and it can stop us from moving forward out of fear of repeating the negative past. So, in my case, I had a subconscious fear of being persecuted again, which was stopping me from moving forward to protect me from being harmed again. But, it was also stopping me from reaching the goal of sharing Michael's important messages. Not reaching this goal, due to my fear, left me immobile and somewhat depressed.

As I cleared my past-life issues and my emotional blocks, I more effortlessly moved forward, and I started feeling better and better about myself and the work that I was to do. Clearing those memories turned everything around. Had I not known about the subconscious as well as spiritual healing, I am not sure where I would have ended up and if I would have gotten the work out. It is very depressing when you're called to do something, but you can't speak your truth, and you can't take the steps necessary to succeed.

I noticed years ago, when I was working at Paramount Pictures, many people called to network with me. I was curious as to why it seemed easier for me to get a job and succeed there than it was for others. When I spoke with them, they appeared to be struggling in more ways than just to get a job at the Studio. In my search for understanding, I learned about the law of attraction.

Like attracts like. When you put out good thoughts, you get good results. So, I learned the techniques to intentionally use the law of attraction to manifest what I desired. And, I realized for myself that it was effortless in certain areas, but I struggled in other ones.

I also started teaching the law of attraction, and I noticed that you could apply the same techniques, or steps, and sometimes it would work, and sometime it wouldn't. It was always consistent in one area of life where it would flow and in other areas it wouldn't.

So, at that point, I realized there must be a block from within in the areas where there was a challenge, so I looked for a solution. That is when I was introduced to a spiritual-healing process called "Ho'oponopono", a Hawaiian term, which means to correct and set right. It's an ancient spiritual process that was once done among the family or group of individuals connected with a particular problem.

It has since updated to be done directly between the individual and Divinity or God. The idea was to repent, ask for forgiveness, be grateful, and return to a place of love. I learned that process and used it daily. When Michael came to me and asked me to write the book, he also asked me to join him in a healing practice. I then discovered I also had a gift for healing. During a healing session, I would intuitively identify the causal level of a problem or situation.

Then, I would clear it using this tool and my gift to help either myself or my clients release the actual cause.

We have an emotional component where we're attached to what happened, to what went wrong and possibly a fear of letting that memory and emotion go, so we hold on. That is what causes a block, and that block can cause a depression. By clearing the cause, the memory, emotions, and blocks, the emotional component as well as any depression, can be released.

TIPS FOR OTHER ENTREPRENEURS

Focus on living in the NOW. When you're in the NOW, you're not dragging in your past negatively coloring or influencing your present moment. You, therefore, also help avoid negatively impacting your future because you're not projecting ideas into the future thoughts like "What if this doesn't happen?" Or, "Am I going to make it?"

One way to do that is to stop the self-limiting talk that comes up because you are worried about your future. Realize that if fears and concerns are coming up that they are mostly based on memories.

Those memories can be from the beginning of time or they could stem from incidents that occurred in this lifetime. It doesn't matter. The subconscious is the part that will hold on to the memory and live out of that over and over again and will continue projecting out from it until those memories and emotions are released.

So, if you can let go in those moments and remind yourself that "It's only a memory" and that you have the ability to move forward if you let go of it, you'll feel better.

And, learn to live from your heart rather than out of your head. The head often retrieves the information from the past to view the world and make decisions. When you operate from the heart, especially from the present moment, you can access more possibilities. You can connect to the all-knowing from the heart and experience more hope. When in the heart, it is easier to experience balance and love.

Also, always come from a place of love. When you view yourself and others, as well as any situation, from a place of love, it is harder to feel depressed. It is much easier to feel positive and hopeful from a place of love.

Joy Pedersen is an International Bestselling Author, Founder and President of Express Success LLC, Doctor of Divinity, Licensed Spiritual Healer, and Certified Spiritual Health Coach serving a primarily international business and professional clientele helping them identify and solve the cause of their personal and business issues.

As an intuitive and gifted healer, Dr. Joy tunes into the subconscious, as well as past lives, to identify and release the hidden causes of negative mindset and emotions to improve relationships, money, business, and well-being. As a spokesperson for Heaven, she shares messages from God, angels and others.

BUSINESSES COME, BUSINESSES GO
BY RUFINA JAMES

MY STORY

Quite some time ago, before I became an entrepreneur, I was a teacher in the California school system. Before that, I used to teach at the university level, but in California they don't provide benefits, so I took a job teaching in the elementary school system; the insurance was great.

But, I found out that the doctors were pretty clueless. And, I had some health problems, so I had to look into the reasons for them myself. During that time, I was teaching, but it was exhausting for me.

One of the things that the State of California decided to do—because the State was getting such an influx of children from other countries who did not speak English and the teachers did not know how to teach them—the children were not passing their tests—was deciding to implement a rule that all California teachers had to have the language-development credential, in order to maintain their teaching credential. This means you had to pass the test or you would lose your job.

You can imagine this created a really difficult problem for a lot of teachers. They had to take classes—night classes or all-day Saturday classes—to take that test. And, the test was not easy. I was one of those teachers. I went to those classes and I sat through these long, boring lectures. Some lecturer would be on the stage giving these dry, boring lectures while they were teaching us about alternative learning methods like super learning, incorporating more movement into your teaching, doing all kinds of fun stuff in the classroom. But, what they were doing was incredibly boring, dry and academic.

We complained and complained. Many people who took the tests flunked. So, they had to take it again. There were three chances.

I passed the test. And I thought, these guys are having such a hard time, and their livelihood depends upon passing the test. In fact, a lot of these teachers were older, and if they lost their credential, they would lose their job and their retirement with it. That was not really fair. So, I wanted to help them, and thought, "How can we do this? They're teaching us about super learning. Super learning is a good thing. So, I wanted to try an experiment which was: put the key learning points on an audio to super-learning music, using the pacing that super learning suggests and doing it in a way that super learning teaches you to do.

So, that's what I did. I would teach all week and come home exhausted. I would sit down and start typing up my narrative. I would choose everything strategically. I did that…day after day…week after week…into the second month and even the third month after coming home from work. I'd going straight to the computer and do this…and I was very tired.

One day, something came over me like a ton of bricks. I looked out the window and said, "Oh, my God, why am I doing this? All these other people are coming home and they're relaxing… or they're able to cook dinner and just sit down for a while… and here I am sitting here at the desk after a long, hard day's work…and I still have lesson plans to do tonight…and I still have papers to correct…and I am sitting here doing this work…and it's possible that no one will even appreciate it. It may not help anybody…what am I thinking?"

It was this *massive* doubt that came over me and the fear that all my work was going to come to nothing. It hit me really hard. I just sat there paralyzed, staring out the window going, "Should I continue? Maybe it's a total waste of time."

> There has to be a part of you that stands back and says, 'This is my goal. What is the simplest way that I can reach it?'

FINDING MY WAY OUT

I kind of snapped out of it after a long time, and I said to myself, "Wait a minute, I'm sitting here. So, either I'm not wasting time or I should walk away from it and not continue." I thought about it for a while. And I thought, "Okay, I've put a whole lot of work into this. Do I want to throw it away or should I see it through? I think this is going to help people, but I had no guarantee. This is the moment of decision, because I can't go on feeling this way. I either make myself go on and finish or I give it up. And so I made a decision, "Alright, I've put too much into this, and the people do need help, so I'm going to finish."

I was still carrying those doubts—they didn't really go away—but I carried on regardless. So, I finished it; and, I spent the money that it took to record it all, edited the thing, and put it together. I had already talked to Super Learning and made an agreement to use their music, so that worked out. And, I did it; we put the audio out and it sold like hot cakes. It was just amazing. And, it was not an expensive tape. It was only $15.00, so it wasn't a big expense. Plus, people needed it. People would call at all hours saying, "I failed the test twice. If I don't pass it I'm going to lose everything!" And then, we started to get people writing to us and telling us they passed!

So, it was a wonderful experience because what I wanted to achieve actually came true. And, we also made a ton of money. So, that was my first experience at business, and it was great.

Eventually the State incorporated all the learning into their university programs, so they didn't have to have the test any more. So, that was the end of the business. And, of course, there was a great loss.

The process of getting over it was to face reality. The business was over. I wasn't able to revive it because things had changed. It was out of my control. That was a big lesson for me. It helped me understand that it was better for me to have a business that was in my control.

(When I went into that business, I knew that it wasn't a permanent thing. I knew that the State was going to change the rules. So, it wasn't a shock. I kind of looked at it as, "Wow, I had this big bonus for several years and now I have to do something else.")

There was, of course, "What am I going to do now?" So, I started another business.

That was when I decided to go into the health field. I started my newsletter. That was a good thing for me to do, too. But, once I got on the Internet there was a big learning curve. The next few years were taken up with a lot of learning about how to make things work.

The newsletter went on for 15 years, and then the FTC (Federal Trade Commission) became extremely concerned about alternative-health claims on the Internet. It's basically because big pharma has a lot of power. They don't want people to use alternative remedies; they would much rather you go and spend it on pharmaceuticals.

So, I needed to start something new again. Certainly, there's always that fear of going into something new.

I am writing a new book. I have not written this kind of book before. Because this is about my own experience, I'm feeling kind of raw. Like, "Wow, do I really want to say all this? Do I want to mention my medical conditions? So, everyone can know them? I am hesitating because I'm a private person. So it's a little scary…no, it's a *lot* scary for me.

TIPS FOR OTHER ENTREPRENEURS

To be resilient during changing tides, set up a way of operating…develop a flexibility.

The way to look at it is… it's just a business. I put a lot of myself into every business that I've done. But, the business isn't me.

I like to learn. That's important. A lot of people don't like to learn and if you don't like to learn you really can't do business on the Internet, because *man*, the Internet keeps changing.

Pick the most important things. You can't learn everything. So, go to the sources that can tell you what is the most important thing now.

You also have to go with what your interests are.

Think through the business and really find out what the marketing plan is and how you can make money with it.

If it really feels right, then you go there. Sometimes, it doesn't feel right for the wrong reasons—sometimes you're just scared, sometimes it's just mind chatter when it really is a good thing. And sometimes, it really isn't a good thing. And, that's hard to sort out.

There are so many distractions on line. You can get so lost. It's a never-ending battle online. Oh my gosh!

Don't give up. It's old advice. There has to be a part of you that stands back and says, "This is my goal. What is the simplest way that I can reach it? This message would be very useful, but what are its limitations?"

Then, I actually research that. I go on forums and find out what people are saying. In many cases, there's a lot of commentary. People have tried it, their experience, the pros, the cons, the failures, the successes. Not always, but you can often get an idea of what it's best for.

A lot of webinars don't tell you what their system is specifically best for. They say it's good for everything. Many people are going to be depressed if they don't understand what I just said…and they're going to lose a lot of money. And they'll be more depressed. They can invest in this course or that course, put a lot of time into it…and the whole thing falls apart. So, people have to be smart about it and understand the pitfalls of entrepreneurship.

Rufina James has been in the health field for 20 years and was the Publisher of the "Real Essential Health Newsletter" for 15 years. She's currently working on a book on her experience and results with a Medical Medium Detox Diet and support group. You can find out more about that at www.superfoodsdetox.com.

NEXT STEPS

STEP #1

If you didn't get your two **FREE** Special Reports to help you navigate through depression in the front of the book, do it now. You'll receive:

1. *50 Reasons You Might Be Depressed In Your Business, (Some Will Even Make You Laugh),* Special Report By Ellen Violette
2. *3 Universal Laws to Help You Deal with Depression* By Jillian Coleman Wheeler

Click Here
(If you have trouble with the link, you may access it directly at: www.overcomingdepressionforentrepreneurs.com/bonus-reports

STEP #2

Join our Facebook Group: Overcoming Depression for Entrepreneurs for sharing, inspiration, prayer askings for tough situations (if you believe in it), and on-going support http://www.Facebook.com/groups/overcomingdepressionforentrepreneurs

STEP #3

Visit the bonus-gift site to get all the extra gifts that many of the contributors have waiting for your! (They are all listed on the next page.)

BONUS GIFTS FROM THE EXPERTS

To access all the bonus gifts:
Click Here
or go to: http://ellenlikes.com/book-buyers-gifts

1. *10 Steps to Running a Thriving Business Without Losing Your Creative Spark!* FREE Special Report
From Literary Strategist and Publishing/Business Expert, Ellen Violette
(Value $10)
If you find that being an entrepreneur gets in the way of your creativity, get my report on how to keep it alive!

2. *Online Superstar Strategies Complimentary Consultation*
From Literary Strategist and Publishing/Business Expert, Ellen Violette
(Value $250)
I'll help you tap into your genius, highlight your creativity and show you how to simplify your business, make more money, and spend more of your time doing what you love in this *free* 30-minute session.

3. *Five Finance Essentials Resources Guide*
From financial expert, Benita Tyler.
(Value $10)
This report for business owners who are ready to feel more prepared to manage profits and make wise choices with finances.

4. *Brainstorming Session*
From Twitter expert, Gary Loper
(Value $125)
One of my brainstorm ideas potentially could increase your business by thousands of dollars. You have absolutely nothing to lose, and have everything to gain, so take advantage of my *free* offer, 30-minute coaching call.

5. Blast Away Your Blocks to Success Complimentary Energy Session

From expert healer, Mary DeYon

(Value $150)

Mary is offering a *free* energy session to remove the trapped emotions that block you from the success you are trying to achieve. Emotionally charged events from your past can still be plaguing you by inhabiting your body with these trapped emotions. This energy healing is done at a distance and can bring more happiness and less worry to you after one session.

6. Life and Language Reports Collection

From NLP expert, Wayne Buckhanan, Ph.D

(Value $32.76)

- *"You Try But"* Report

- *"MnM Goals"* Report

- *"Circle of Excellence"* guided exercise worksheet & audio

As mentioned in the chapter, I have collected a few resources to help you "crush it" in spite of those depressive symptoms that sneak up on us. Here's what you'll find:

- *You Try But* report – Learn about the big three language patterns that we use (and misuse) consistently. By leveraging these three patterns, you'll be better equipped to send yourself in resourceful directions.

- *MnM Goals* report – Explore the distinctions between the types of goals we tend to set in our businesses and those that we may want to set in other areas of our lives. You'll discover how to use "minimal" goals to reach maximal outcomes.

- *Circle of Excellence* guided exercise – This worksheet and audio will walk you through the process of setting up some new triggers that you can use in the heat of the moment to shift into resourceful states and feel good doing it.

You'll also have the opportunity to hear more about how other crazy sounding stuff that comes from cognitive-behavioral psychology can make practical differences in your life.

7. 5-Step Marketing-Action Plan
From Twitter's past Top 100 Entrepreneurs to Watch,
Gerri Chambers
(Value $199)
We'll take an in-depth look at your current online marketing efforts, and I'll give you 5 personalized actions to instantly implement to increase visibility, authority and sales in this 30-minute coaching session.

8. *"You Got This, Girl!" Video and Scriptures*

From filmmaker and Christian children's author, Kim Thornton

(Value $17)

Inspirational video and scriptures that will lift women's spirits as they go on with their business and access to her free Facebook group to inspire them daily.

9. *10 Ways to Feel Better Right Now Special Report*

From depression expert, Jillian Coleman Wheeler

(Value $39)

Think of it as your quick-start guide to healing depression. It's all about helping you feel better, and supporting you in healing your depression permanently. Please remember, you are not alone.

10. *2020 VISION, Beyond Vision Boards*

From Betsy M. Hall

(Value $225.00)

In this session, we'll align with the Divine, journal your dreams, and strategize next steps. We'll also plan growth in the areas of relationships, profession and creativity.

11. *Stress Assessment Consultation*

From stress-management expert, Brooklyn Reyes.

(Value $250)

Find out if your stress level is holding you back at work or in life. Your *free* 30-minute assessment will also include a 30-day action plan!

12. *Take Back Your Life! Relax with Self-Hypnosis and Feel Your Stress Melt Away"* **FREE Special Report**

From spiritual healer, Joy Pedersen

(Value $10)

5 simple steps to reduce stress, gain control over your emotions, and find inner peace with self-hypnosis.

13. *10 Questions You Must Answer Before You Start a Successful Superfood Detox.*

Rufina James

(Value $10)

Answer these 10 Questions to help you decide if going on a superfoods detox is right for you.

CONNECT WITH THE EXPERTS

Ellen Violette:

http://www.booksbusinessabundance.com

Email: ellen@booksbusinessabundance.com

Social Media:

http://www.facebook.com/groups/overcomingdepressionforentrepreneurs

http://www.facebook.com/groups/selfpublishingcommunity

Benita Tyler

www.womancfo.com

Social Media:

Facebook: www.facebook.com/womancfo

Instagram: instagram.com@womancfo

Gary Loper

http://www.GaryLoper.com

Social Media:

https://twitter.com/GaryLoper

Julia Neiman

http://www.MonetizeYourPassionAcademy.com

Email: Julia@MonetizeYourPassionAcademy.com

Wayne Buckhanan

https://mercs.net

Mary DeYon

www.MaryDeyon.com

Email: Mary@MaryDeyon.com

Gerri Milligan

WOAMTEC

(A professional women's networking groups)

@woamtecsugarland

Kim Thornton

http://Heisreel.com

Email: Kimthornton19@bellsouth.net

Social Media:

https://www.facebook.com/kimheisreel

http://www.facebook.com/helpingwomenovercomedepression

Jillian Coleman Wheeler

http://www.helpfordepressionbook.com

Email: jill@rebootbliss.com

Willie Crawford

http://www.williecrawford.com

Betsy Hall

http://www.mastermindstoday.com

Email: Betsy@betsy-hall.com

Rick Cooper

http://www.SocialMediaOutcomes.com

Brooklyn Reyes

http://www.stressbusterhandbook.com

Christen Violette

Email: Christen@createasplash.com

Mary Latela

http://www.mlatelablog.wordpress.com

Email: mlatela@outlook.com

Joy Pedersen

http://www.expresssuccess.net

Email:Info@expresssuccess.net

Rufina James

http://www.superfoodsdetox.com

RESOURCES

Web MD: Depression Resources
https://www.webmd.com/depression/guide/depression-resources#1

Better Help
Convenient, affordable, private counseling online
https://www.betterhelp.com/

Hope for Depression Research Foundation
www.hopefordepression.org

This organization funds cutting-edge scientific research into the origins, diagnosis, treatment, and prevention of depression and its related mood and other emotional disorders-bipolar disorder, postpartum depression, post-traumatic stress syndrome, anxiety disorder and suicide.

hdrf@hopefordepression.org

212 6763200

ACKNOWLEDGEMENTS

First, I want to thank all my co-contributors, this book would not have been possible without your amazing stories.

I also want to give a special thanks to Betsy M. Hall who helped me figure out all the logistics of getting this book done and for loving me just the way I am, supporting me in being my best self, and being there to tell me when I'm wrong when I am, but with love, always with love.

To Jillian Coleman Wheeler for your love and friendship and brilliant writing and editing. I am continually in awe of you!

To Joie Gharrity for believing in the project and creating awesome graphics for it! And, Mary Boiselle for all her organizational help.

To Tanya Schupp, Karl May, and Kristy-Lea Tritz for your web support.

To Alex Branning, Jeff Hunter, and Willie Crawford for your marketing advice.

To my community-the reason I do what I do.

To my family, I love you.

And most of all to my husband, who has been there through the ups and the downs, who has always believed in me, and thinks I'm brilliant!

ABOUT ELLEN VIOLETTE

Ellen Violette helps Founders & CEO's, Speakers, Consultants, Coaches, and Entrepreneurs increase their influence in their respective industries through the process of creating a book, launching it #1 bestseller, and using it to make a even bigger impact in the world.

She's an award-winning book and business coach, a 3-time eLit Award winner, former regular contributor to Published! Magazine and host of the Books Business Abundance Podcast.

She is a multiple #1 best-selling author and has written several books, including: *Turn Your Book into 10K Clients, 5 Keys to a High-Income Business; Real Easy eBooks, 8 Ways to Write or Repurpose Content into a Bestseller; Real Easy eBooks Workbook, A Step -By-Step Guide to Take Your eBook From Idea* to Bestseller; How to Make Money Writing Quick Non-Fiction eBooks ...Guaranteed; 21 Simple Strategies to Jumpstart Your Book Marketing Online, Proven Techniques for Quick Results; and more!

She is also the co-author of *Sell More eBooks, Low & No-Cost Tactics to EXPLODE Your eBook Sales And Downloads* with Internet Pioneer, Jim Edwards as well as a contributor to three collaboration #1 International bestsellers.

She is also the creator of the groundbreaking programs *3 Days to eBook Cash and Bestseller eBook Launch Secrets, Bestseller Book-Title Secrets* and *Rapid Book Creation Secrets* and more!

And, she's a Grammy-nominated songwriter, and producer.

As a personal coach, multiple #1 bestseller author, and product creator, Ellen is on a mission to help heal the world one person, one book, and one business at a time. She has helped thousands of people around the world spread their message and change lives including their own! She currently lives in San Diego with her husband, David "Christen" Violette.

www.ingramcontent.com/pod-product-compliance
Lightning Source LLC
Chambersburg PA
CBHW030629220526
45463CB00004B/1456